PRAISE FOR *TAX-FREE INCOME FOR LIFE*

"*Tax-Free Income for Life* is one of the most important books in the pioneering tax-free retirement planning paradigm to date. It's the only book of its kind to address market risk, tax rate risk, and longevity risk within one powerful, comprehensive strategy. It's a must read for those preparing for a happy and prosperous retirement."

—Brian Hanson, Hanson Wealth
Management, Eden Prairie, Minn.

"Finally, a book that puts the whole plan together! This book covers every issue a retiree may face and how to plan for it. Planning for retirement is complex, but this book gives step-by-step guidance, and ties everything together in a way that is easy to understand."

—Jennifer Baker, CFP, CPA, RICP,
Baker Wealth Strategies, Houston

"This book's message couldn't be more timely! These revolutionary principles are laid out in a digestible format while underscoring the need to work with an experienced and qualified financial professional. *Tax-Free Income for Life* is going to reshape the way you plan your retirement!"

—Jeffrey Tamas, CFFM, FIC,
Ideal Retirement Solutions, Port Charlotte, Fla.

"As a CPA, I realize that the more you can eliminate risk, the better chance you have to succeed in anything you do. This book is a must read for those who want to reduce the financial risks they will be facing in retirement, so they can live a more prosperous life."

—Dave Hall, CPA, Etrends Group, Collierville, Tenn.

"David McKnight's new book lays out an actionable plan for sustainable retirement income throughout retirement. In this follow-up to *The Power of Zero*, he explains why tax-free guaranteed lifetime income is an indispensable part of every retirement plan. It's a message that drives home the importance of working with a professional financial adviser to keep your plan on track. Well done!"

—Craig W. Jergenson, CFP, Coach Craig
Financial, Maple Grove, Minn.

"Most Americans underestimate tax rate risk along with myriad other retirement risks. This book not only shows you how to mitigate these threats, but does so in plain English, providing solid, comprehensive, and easy-to-understand solutions."

—Robert M. Ryerson, CFP,
New Century Planning, Waldwick, N.J.

"David has done it again! His understanding of what pre-retirees and retirees are looking for in a comprehensive retirement strategy is unparalleled in our industry. In this book, he adeptly lays out an objective approach to successfully navigating the opportunities and pitfalls leading up to and through one's retirement years. This is a must read for consumers and financial professionals alike."

—Shawn Sigler, MSM, CLTC, Financial
Independence Group, Cornelius, N.C.

"If you've read David McKnight's other bestselling books, this one ties it all together with a step-by-step approach to building a risk-proof retirement plan. Inside is the complete formula. A *must read*!"

—Victoria Larson,
Vitality Investments, Sarasota, Fla.

"More than ever, retirees are at risk of running out of money prematurely. David McKnight lays out advanced planning strategies that, when implemented properly, will protect your wealth and provide more dependable retirement income."

—Lane G. Martinsen, author of
The Holistic Retirement Planning Revolution

TAX-FREE INCOME FOR LIFE

TAX-FREE INCOME FOR LIFE

*A Step-by-Step Plan
for a Secure Retirement*

David McKnight

PORTFOLIO / PENGUIN

PORTFOLIO /PENGUIN

An imprint of Penguin Random House LLC

penguinrandomhouse.com

Most Portfolio books are available at a discount when purchased in quantity for sales promotions or corporate use. Special editions, which include personalized covers, excerpts, and corporate imprints, can be created when purchased in large quantities. For more information, please call (212) 572-2232 or email specialmarkets@penguinrandomhouse.com. Your local bookstore can also assist with discounted bulk purchases using the Penguin Random House corporate Business-to-Business program. For assistance in locating a participating retailer, email B2B@penguinrandomhouse.com.

LIBRARY OF CONGRESS CATALOGING-IN-PUBLICATION DATA

Names: McKnight, David C., author.

Title: Tax-free income for life : a step-by-step plan

for a secure retirement / David McKnight.

Description: New York : Portfolio, [2020] |

Identifiers: LCCN 2020032035 (print) | LCCN 2020032036 (ebook) |

ISBN 9780593327753 (hardcover) | ISBN 9780593327760 (ebook)

Subjects: LCSH: Retirement income—Planning. | Finance, Personal. |

Retirement—Planning. | Investments.

Classification: LCC HG179 .M25124 2020 (print) | LCC HG179 (ebook) |

DDC 332.024/014—dc23

LC record available at https://lccn.loc.gov/2020032035

LC ebook record available at https://lccn.loc.gov/2020032036

Printed in the United States of America

5th Printing

To my mother,
who has always believed in me.

CONTENTS

FOREWORD

David McKnight doesn't have a crystal ball, but he can see the future. He sees the consequences of unfunded liabilities for programs like Social Security, Medicare, Medicaid, and government pensions and knows that someday soon that massive bill will come due. Because of recent events, that day of reckoning will come even sooner than you think. As I write this, Congress just passed a $2 trillion stimulus package in response to the COVID-19 pandemic. Word is, even more stimulus bills are in the works. And how is all this spending going to be financed? You guessed it—even more debt. Folks, the tax freight train that is bearing down on your retirement plan just picked up a little more speed! Who is going to pay this tax bill when it arrives? Billionaires? Major corporations? Nope, it's going to be everyday Americans like you and me.

You may think you know how much is in your 401(k) or IRA, but unless you can predict what tax rates will be when you take that money out, you don't really know how much money you will have. Let's face it, if you have a tax-deferred retirement account, you are in a partnership with the federal government and *they* get to determine how much you get to spend in retirement.

For years, David has been crisscrossing the country, warning everyday Americans about the tax freight train bearing down on them, and the importance of investing in tax-free accounts. I got to know David during the filming of Doug Orchard's documentary *The Power of Zero: The Tax Train Is Coming*. If you haven't seen that movie, I recommend it to you. Economists from the most prestigious universities across the country share their research on our country's growing debt crisis and its impact on future tax rates. I have personally moved more of my wealth to tax-free accounts, including life insurance, because of David's message about the dangers of higher taxes.

In *Tax-Free Income for Life*, David raises a warning cry about a second risk I've been telling Americans about my entire career: longevity risk. This risk is so insidious because it magnifies all the other risks you'll be facing in retirement: *sequence-of-return risk*, *withdrawal rate risk*, *long-term care risk*, and *inflation risk*. When it comes to sound retirement planning, you can't just think about market returns. You have to start managing longevity risk!

The antidote to longevity risk is guaranteed lifetime inflation-adjusted income. Look, I've been studying lifetime income for thirty years and have written five books about the subject, and here's what the math and science show: a successful retirement is not about asset allocation, diversification, or rates of return. That was critical during your accumulation phase. During your retirement years, it's all about covering basic lifestyle expenses with guaranteed inflation-adjusted income designed to last for the rest of your life. In retirement, it's not about assets, it's about income!

Folks, a successful retirement is rarely a do-it-yourself project. So take the time to read this book and meet with a qualified, experienced financial professional. By making a few simple tweaks to your portfolio now, you can reduce your future tax bill *and* make sure your retirement income lasts for the rest of your life.

Tom Hegna
author, speaker, economist, PBS host
www.tomhegna.com
March 26, 2020

TAX-FREE INCOME FOR LIFE

Chapter 1

THE TWO GREAT
RETIREMENT RISKS

You've invested diligently your entire life, scrimping and saving at every turn, all in anticipation of this very moment. You're ready to embark upon the longest permanent, self-imposed period of unemployment in your lifetime. It could last twenty-five, thirty-five, heck, who knows, maybe even forty years if you keep eating your Mueslix. But are you ready to go the distance? How likely are you to remain safely ensconced in that blissful state of willful unemployment? Are there unseen risks that could cut the vacation short, catapulting you back into the workforce at the most inopportune time in your life?

Two major risks loom large on the retirement landscape, threatening to derail the retirement plans of even the most diligent and cautious of retirees. Economists and retirement experts have spent years researching math-based strategies that address each risk separately, but they have yet to devise a unified strategy that mitigates the cumulative effects of *both* risks in a meaningful way. As a result, the vast majority of Americans feel some sense of angst as they venture into their retirement years.

THE FIRST GREAT RETIREMENT RISK

If you've read *The Power of Zero,* you're well acquainted with the first risk of which I speak: *tax rate risk.* This is a risk worth revisiting, because the threat has only compounded since the publication of the updated and revised version of the book in 2018. The risk that tax rates even ten years from now will be dramatically higher is all the more real today than it was even two years ago.

I've made the case in *The Power of Zero,* on *The Power of Zero Show,* and in the movie *The Power of Zero: The Tax Train Is Coming* that because of our nation's skyrocketing debt, higher taxes are inevitable and will be making a visit to your retirement plan in the very near future.

For years, the bearer of this bad news was former comptroller general of the federal government David Walker. Back in 2009, when the national debt was "*only*" $10 trillion, he was running around the country with his hair on fire

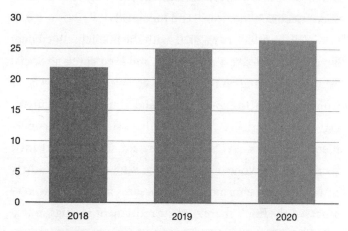

US NATIONAL DEBT

Figures are in trillions of dollars.*

making the case that the fiscal condition of our country was precarious at best, and destined for bankruptcy at worst. His Fiscal Wake-up Tour took him to college campuses across the country and ultimately landed him on *60 Minutes,* where he warned of the need to dramatically reform our nation's entitlement programs to avoid the bankrupting of America. He even made an Oscar-nominated movie about the nation's debt crisis, called *I.O.U.S.A.* In 2011 he wrote a *CNN* op-ed that made the case that tax rates in our country would have to double in order to service the na-

* "United States Government Debt 1942–2020 Data: 2021–2022 Forecast: Historical," Trading Economics, https://tradingeconomics.com/united-states/government-debt.

tional debt *and* deliver on entitlement programs such as Social Security, Medicare, and Medicaid.

Well, here we are in 2020, with the publicly stated debt having ballooned to $26.5 trillion and Medicare and Social Security teetering on the brink of collapse, and all we hear from the media, the government, and a huge swath of financial experts is crickets. It's a truth that's simply too inconvenient to address. As David Walker said, it's the "dirty little secret that everyone in Washington knows." And this dirty little secret has enormous repercussions for retirees who've amassed the lion's share of their retirement savings in tax-deferred vehicles like 401(k)s and IRAs.

Fortunately, a few forward-thinking advocates in academia understand the math behind our nation's fiscal woes and have begun to amplify their warning cries to America. One of those lone prophets in the wilderness is Dr. Laurence Kotlikoff, of Boston University. He's the foremost expert on an accountancy method known as fiscal gap accounting, an approach used by nearly every developed country in the world except—wait for it—the United States. Fiscal gap accounting projects a nation's expenses (including benefits they're required to pay by law) over a period of seventy-five years. It then compares those expenses to the country's anticipated revenue over that same time frame. Is there a difference between what your country has promised in the form of programs, benefits, and services versus what it can actually deliver? If so, then your country has a fiscal gap. And that fiscal gap is your *true* national debt.

In order to quantify the fiscal gap for the United States, Dr. Kotlikoff calculated the net present value of the United States' future financial shortfall (i.e., the difference between what we've promised and what we can actually afford to pay over the next seventy-five years) and has drawn a disturbing conclusion. Our true national debt isn't $26.5 trillion, it's closer to $239 trillion. In other words, we'd have to have $239 trillion sitting in a savings account today earning treasury rates, just to be able to deliver on all those promises. It's worth noting that Dr. Kotlikoff revised this number upward from $221 trillion in 2018. The burden of our nation's true debt load, it seems, is accelerating at breakneck speed.

I've often sparred with online "financial experts" who claim that all this talk about debt is much ado about nothing. It's unnecessary fearmongering. After all, our debt-to-GDP ratio is only around 106 percent. It was worse after World War II and we managed to claw our way back from that! Here's the difference: In the immediate wake of WWII, the true debt-to-GDP ratio *was* around 110 percent—not far from the official publicly stated debt-to-GDP ratio today. But when the fiscal condition of our country is viewed through the lens of fiscal gap accounting, our nation's debt-to-GDP ratio today is revealed to be *much* higher than it was following WWII. Dr. Kotlikoff puts it much closer to 1,000 percent. To put this into perspective for you, the next closest country (that actually *does* practice true fiscal gap accounting) is Japan, clocking in at "only" 250 percent. In other words, our financial outlook is four times as dire as that of the next worst country in the world. If this were a race toward insolvency, we'd be winning by a landslide!

Yet those same online gurus continue to protest. According to these "experts," when the time comes to make good on all these unfunded promises, we'll simply print our way out of it! We'll return to seventies-style inflation in order to keep our promises to America's baby boomers. Here's what these financial gurus fail to appreciate: Social Security, Medicare, and Medicaid are all tied to inflation. When you print more money, inflation goes up, and the cost of these programs rises commensurately. So by printing more money, you aren't really solving the problem. You're just growing the cost of these programs at the very same rate at which you grow the supply of money.

Others affirm that we'll continue to borrow more and more money from countries such as China. As with printing money, there's a fatal problem with this approach. Eventually our debt will get so big that we risk a sovereign debt crisis. This is when other countries stop loaning us money because they don't believe we can pay it back. Many economists agree that the canary in the coal mine for a sovereign debt crisis is when we begin running a trillion-dollar deficit. As of the time of this writing, the federal budget is $4.6 trillion and projected tax revenues are $3.6 trillion. In other words, the trillion-dollar deficit is already upon us! As you can see, neither printing money nor borrowing our way out of our current debt crisis is a sound, responsible long-term solution to our problems.

So if we can't print our way out of our problems and we can't borrow our way out, what's the solution? A growing contingent of economists believe we will eventually have to tax our way out of our problems. Before filmmaker Doug Orchard and I filmed *The Power of Zero*, I was reasonably confident that tax rates would have to rise dramatically in the next ten years to keep our country solvent. But after we finished interviewing dozens of experts in academia and government think tanks, politicians, and industry experts, I became absolutely convinced that tax rates would *have* to rise dramatically *in the next ten years* to avoid fiscal insolvency. Mathematically, we've passed the point of no return.

In our movie we interviewed former secretary of state George Shultz, Utah governor Gary Herbert, national IRA expert Ed Slott, former comptroller general David Walker, and a host of professors from the most prestigious universities across the country. They're all reading the same music and they're all singing the same song. If we don't change the fiscal course of our country today, and in dramatic fashion, tax rates will have to rise precipitously by 2030. Some of these experts even used the d-word as it relates to the future of tax rates. That's right, tax rates would have to *double* just to keep our country solvent.

THE SECOND GREAT RETIREMENT RISK

If tax rate risk isn't enough to put a knot of angst in the pit of your stomach, then the second major retirement risk will almost certainly finish the job. This insidious threat to your retirement plan is known as *longevity risk*. Simply put, it's the risk of running out of money before you die. You know, having too much life at the end of your money. Living too long and dying broke. Thanks to advances in medical technology that allow Americans to live longer and longer lives, longevity risk is becoming all the more acute. Most retirement experts today say it's not enough to plan for only a twenty-year retirement. They're running retirement projections out to age one hundred and beyond.

The reason longevity risk is so dangerous is because it magnifies and enhances a subset of risks that are traditionally responsible for people running out of money before they die. I'm referring to sequence-of-return risk, withdrawal rate risk, long-term care risk, and inflation risk (more on these in chapter two). If you're planning on living only five years, none of these risks are likely to land you in the poorhouse. But a traditional retirement may last anywhere from twenty to forty years. And the longer your retirement lasts, the higher the statistical likelihood that one of these risks could send your retirement plan cartwheeling off the tracks. Essentially, there's more time for bad stuff to happen during a thirty-year retirement than during a ten-year retirement.

Some retirement experts insist that the only way for you to vanquish these retirement risks is to save more money. In other words, build more cushion into your retirement plan during your working years so you can be über-prepared to weather any financial storm in retirement. You know, throw more money at the problem! But how much additional money will you need to fully neutralize these four risks? It's hard to say because the single most important variable in the retirement calculus is a complete unknown: how long you're going to live! Whether you realize it or not, longevity risk is likely to play a starring role in the success or failure of your retirement plan.

No problem, you might be thinking. I'll just look at the median life expectancy for someone my age and plan accordingly. Here's the problem: *median* life expectancy doesn't predict your *actual* life expectancy. It simply predicts the point in time by which half the people your age will have died. The other half are going to live longer—in some cases, much longer.

For years, our industry has poked and prodded thousands of respondents to get a measure of their concern for longevity risk. According to a recent survey by a major financial services company, 85 percent of retirees feel financially anxious and 89 percent would rather have financial security over the long term than cash in hand today. Yet only 44 percent of respondents said they were doing anything to address the financial implications of living longer.*

These statistics reinforce what I'm hearing as I speak around the country to thousands of private investors, financial planners, organizations, and corporations: there's increasing anxiety that no matter how much you save, you are likely to run out of money in retirement.

This anxiety is further reinforced by a recent study by Harvard Business School.† In the most comprehensive

---

* Javier Simon, "Research Finds Americans Seek Financial Advice but Lack Planning," Planadviser, September 14, 2016, https://www.planadviser.com/research-finds-americans-seek-financial-advice-but-lack-planning/.

† Peter Cohan, "This Harvard Study of 4,000 Millionaires Revealed Something Surprising About Money and Happiness," Inc., December 14, 2017, https://www.inc.com/peter-cohan/will-10-million-make-you-happier-harvard-says-yes-if-you-make-it-yourself-give-it-away.html.

study of its kind, researchers interviewed four thousand pre-retirees, each with a net worth of at least $1 million, in an attempt to answer the age-old question "How much money is enough?" Did the respondents feel secure with their present level of net worth? If not, what amount of money would it take to spur a greater sense of security? The results may startle you. For those who had $1 million, it wasn't enough. They needed closer to $2 million to be satisfied. Those who had $2 million needed closer to $4 million. For those with $4 million, $8 million was their magic number. It wasn't until researchers started surveying those with a net worth of $15 million or more that they began to see consistently stable levels of satisfaction. So, how much is enough? According to Harvard Business School, it's about $15 million. Anything short of that and you're likely to feel some level of insecurity about how long your assets will last in retirement. What this book will show is that you don't need $15 million to have a secure retirement; you just need a rock-solid strategy to mitigate the two greatest risks that threaten to derail your retirement plan.

BUT HOW DO YOU MITIGATE
TAX RATE RISK *AND* LONGEVITY RISK?

In *The Power of Zero*, I laid out a plan to fully mitigate the impact of tax rate risk. In an environment of rising tax rates, you need to have the mathematically perfect amount of money in your taxable and tax-deferred buckets. Everything above and beyond those ideal amounts should be systematically repositioned to your tax-free bucket. If you've embraced the asset-shifting approach in *The Power of Zero*, then you're well on your way to neutralizing the impact of tax rate risk.

But what of longevity risk? Can you have your cake and eat it too? Is it possible to completely vanquish tax rate risk *and* longevity risk from your retirement picture? While the concepts in *The Power of Zero* do fully mitigate your first big retirement risk, they don't explicitly address longevity risk. Certainly, giving less money to the IRS over the arc of your retirement can extend the life of your investments. But it doesn't necessarily guarantee fiscal solvency for life. It doesn't *ensure* that your retirement savings will last until you die. So, how do we crack the code? Is there a way to fully mitigate both risks while restoring peace of mind to a generation of retiring Americans? The answer is a resounding yes! By the end of this book you'll have a step-by-step strategy designed to eliminate stress and restore peace to your retirement plan. Granted, this strategy *will* require a bit more complexity than the traditional set-it-and-forget-it approach to retirement planning. But don't worry, there's a massive payoff at the end that will more than reward you for all the extra effort. And remember, when things do veer into the complex, I'll be at your side explaining and clarifying every step along the way.

Tax-Free Income for Life shows you step-by-step how to secure a tax-free income that lasts as long as you do. In chapter two we'll further define the four sub-risks that are threatening your retirement portfolio and demonstrate how longevity risk makes them all the more lethal. Once you understand the extent to which longevity risk can amplify these four risks, you'll stop at nothing to eliminate them from your retirement. Chapter three explores the traditional approach to eliminating longevity risk and why it fails to restore peace and predictability to your retirement plan. I'll also explain why it's far and away the *most* expensive way to mitigate this insidious risk. In chapter four, I'll discuss a proven math-based alternative to neutralizing longevity risk in an effort to optimize your retirement plan. I'll also show you how this approach can help free up hundreds of thousands of dollars for important discretionary expenses over the arc of your retirement. In chapter five, I'll discuss the perceived shortcomings of this math-based approach and explain why most Americans have yet to adopt it. Then I'll show you a revolutionary alternative that mitigates longevity risk in a satisfying way. In chapter six, I'll lay out a strategy that marries the Power of Zero approach to neutralizing tax rate risk with the math-based approach to solving longevity risk in a groundbreaking way. I'll also explain why it's likely you haven't heard of this revolutionary strategy until now. In chapter seven, I'll unveil the final, indispensable component of this comprehensive retirement approach: an innovative investment strategy that minimizes risk and maximizes return in your investment portfolio. Finally, in chapter eight, I'll lay out a step-by-step road map for how to effectively neutralize these two massive risks in your own financial scenario. By the time we're done, you'll have a comprehensive blueprint for how to achieve a *Tax-Free Income for Life* retirement!

What do you say? Are you ready to get started? Are you ready to neutralize the two largest roadblocks to your retirement success? Are you ready to ensure that this permanent period of willful unemployment will never be disrupted? If so, let's get to work!

Chapter 2

THE RISK MULTIPLIER

As I mentioned in chapter one, there are four risks lurk-
ing in your investment portfolio, and it's just a question of time before they crash your retirement party. As
scary as sequence-of-return risk, withdrawal rate risk, long-
term care risk, and inflation risk can be on their own, they're
even more terrifying when amplified by longevity risk. You
see, the longer you live, the greater the likelihood these risks
could send your retirement portfolio into a death spiral
from which it never recovers. Longevity risk is the most
pernicious of all risks because it is a risk multiplier. It compounds or multiplies the likelihood *and* the consequences
of each of the four risks we'll be discussing in this chapter.
Let's take a look at each of these risks one by one so we can

understand the urgency behind creating a plan that purges them from your retirement picture.

SEQUENCE-OF-RETURN RISK

To set the table for our discussion of the first risk, let me describe a scenario that plays out all too often in financial advisory offices across the country:

Jack and Julie Harrison step into their new financial adviser's office, atwitter at the prospect of beginning what they hope will be a thirty-year period of permanent, willful unemployment. They've worked hard and saved even harder, and now they're ready for the big payoff. They can hardly wait to see the results of their adviser's analysis of their retirement picture.

After a few minutes of small talk, the adviser triumphantly pushes a retirement projection across the table. The Harrisons pick it up and begin to pore over it. According to the adviser's calculations, they can draw $65,000 per year from their $1 million IRA every year for 30 years. And all they have to do is *average* 8 percent growth per year. *Piece of cake*, the Harrisons think to themselves. The market has averaged 8 percent per year over the previous 30 years, so why should the next 30 years be any different? Moreover, coupled with their Social Security, that $65,000 completely covers their lifestyle needs. Boom! *Permanent willful unemployment, here we come!* After a few moments of unrestrained euphoria, their eyes home in on the massive number at the bottom of the page. It's the amount they'll have left over by age 95. It's over $2 million! Their eyes nearly pop out of their sockets.

Year	Beginning of Year Account Value	Annual Cash Flow	Earnings Rate	End of Year Account Value
2021	$1,000,000	–$65,000	8.00%	$1,009,800
2022	$1,009,800	–$65,000	8.00%	$1,020,384
2023	$1,020,384	–$65,000	8.00%	$1,031,815
2024	$1,031,815	–$65,000	8.00%	$1,044,160
2025	$1,044,160	–$65,000	8.00%	$1,057,493
2026	$1,057,493	–$65,000	8.00%	$1,071,892
2027	$1,071,892	–$65,000	8.00%	$1,087,443
2028	$1,087,443	–$65,000	8.00%	$1,104,239
2029	$1,104,239	–$65,000	8.00%	$1,122,378
2030	$1,122,387	–$65,000	8.00%	$1,141,968
2031	$1,141,968	–$65,000	8.00%	$1,163,126
2032	$1,163,126	–$65,000	8.00%	$1,185,976

2033	$1,185,976	−$65,000	8.00%	$1,210,654
2034	$1,210,654	−$65,000	8.00%	$1,237,306
2035	$1,237,306	−$65,000	8.00%	$1,266,091
2036	$1,266,091	−$65,000	8.00%	$1,297,178
2037	$1,297,178	−$65,000	8.00%	$1,330,752
2038	$1,330,752	−$65,000	8.00%	$1,367,012
2039	$1,367,012	−$65,000	8.00%	$1,406,173
2040	$1,406,173	−$65,000	8.00%	$1,448,467
2041	$1,448,467	−$65,000	8.00%	$1,494,145
2042	$1,494,145	−$65,000	8.00%	$1,543,476
2043	$1,543,476	−$65,000	8.00%	$1,596,754
2044	$1,596,754	−$65,000	8.00%	$1,654,295
2045	$1,654,295	−$65,000	8.00%	$1,716,438
2046	$1,716,438	−$65,000	8.00%	$1,783,553
2047	$1,783,553	−$65,000	8.00%	$1,856,038
2048	$1,856,038	−$65,000	8.00%	$1,934,321
2049	$1,934,321	−$65,000	8.00%	$2,018,966
2050	$2,018,866	−$65,000	8.00%	$2,110,175

But the financial adviser isn't done. He slides a second projection across the table, scarcely able to contain his enthusiasm. If the Harrisons don't want to leave more than $2 million to the next generation, he explains, they could spend $82,500 per year and bounce the check to the undertaker at age 95.

Year	Beginning of Year Account Value	Annual Cash Flow	Earnings Rate	End of Year Account Value
2021	$1,000,000	–$82,500	8.00%	$990,900
2022	$1,990,900	–$82,500	8.00%	$981,072
2023	$981,072	–$82,500	8.00%	$970,458
2024	$970,458	–$82,500	8.00%	$958,944
2025	$958,994	–$82,500	8.00%	$946,614
2026	$946,614	–$82,500	8.00%	$933,243
2027	$933,243	–$82,500	8.00%	$918,802
2028	$918,802	–$82,500	8.00%	$903,207
2029	$903,207	–$82,500	8.00%	$886,363
2030	$886,363	–$82,500	8.00%	$868,172
2031	$868,172	–$82,500	8.00%	$848,526
2032	$848,526	–$82,500	8.00%	$827,308

2033	$827,308	–$82,500	8.00%	$804,393
2034	$804,393	–$82,500	8.00%	$779,644
2035	$779,644	–$82,500	8.00%	$752,916
2036	$752,916	–$82,500	8.00%	$724,049
2037	$724,049	–$82,500	8.00%	$692,873
2038	$692,873	–$82,500	8.00%	$659,203
2039	$659,203	–$82,500	8.00%	$622,839
2040	$622,839	–$82,500	8.00%	$583,566
2041	$583,566	–$82,500	8.00%	$541,151
2042	$541,151	–$82,500	8.00%	$495,344
2043	$495,344	–$82,500	8.00%	$445,871
2044	$445,871	–$82,500	8.00%	$392,441
2045	$392,441	–$82,500	8.00%	$334,736
2046	$334,736	–$82,500	8.00%	$272,415
2047	$272,415	–$82,500	8.00%	$205,108
2048	$205,108	–$82,500	8.00%	$132,417
2049	$132,417	–$82,500	8.00%	$53,910
2050	$53,910	–$82,500	8.00%	$–30,877

As the Harrisons look over the projection, visions of cruises, daily rounds of golf, and doting on cherubic grandchildren in far-flung cities dance in their heads. They can hardly believe it. For all their retirement dreams to become reality, all they have to do is *average* 8 percent growth per year. As they take in the row of numbers, they both smile broadly. Could it be this simple?

The answer, of course, is that a successful retirement is never this simple. What this financial adviser's projections failed to account for is the real-world nature of stock market returns. Average rates of return can be a meaningful metric in the years leading up to retirement, but they lose all significance the very moment you begin taking distributions from your stock market portfolio. Once distributions begin, the sequence in which those returns are experienced tells a whole different story. When you begin withdrawing money, the rules of the game change dramatically.

To illustrate the importance of sequence-of-return risk in retirement, consider the story of two couples, the Johnsons and the Browns. Both couples start with a $1 million nest egg when they retire at age 65. Both couples take annual $50,000 distributions, with 3 percent annual adjustments for inflation. Throughout their 30-year retirements, both couples *average* a 6.5 percent return on their stock market portfolios.* The Johnsons, however, experience a cluster of negative returns early in retirement, while the Browns experience their negative returns much closer to the end.

The Johnsons Sequence of Returns: Early Losses 6.5% Average Return				The Browns Sequence of Returns: Late Losses 6.5% Average Return		
Net Return	Withdrawal	Balance	Age	Net Return	Withdrawal	Balance
		$1,000,000	65			$1,000,000
−25.1%	$50,000.00	$699,000.00	66	26.4%	$50,000.00	$1,214,000.00
−13.3%	$51,500.00	$554,533.00	67	9.7%	$51,500.00	$1,280,258.00
−5.2%	$53,045.00	$472,652.28	68	14.3%	$53,045.00	$1,410,289.89
4.9%	$54,636.35	$441,175.90	69	6.8%	$54,636.35	$1,451,553.26
13.6%	$56,275.44	$444,900.38	70	16.2%	$56,275.44	$1,630,429.44
−7.1%	$57,963.70	$335,348.75	71	11.4%	$57,963.70	$1,758,334.70
9.3%	$59,702.61	$328,693.57	72	7.3%	$59,702.61	$1,826,990.51
12.2%	$61,493.69	$307,300.49	73	5.1%	$61,493.69	$1,858,673.34
16.5%	$63,338.50	$294,666.56	74	−9.9%	$63,338.50	$1,611,326.17
5.0%	$65,238.66	$244,161.57	75	13.8%	$65,238.66	$1,768,450.53

* Note that the Browns' investment returns occur in the inverse order of the Johnsons' investment returns.

9.4%	$67,195.82	$199.916.57	76	17.6%	$67,195.82	$2,012,502.00
12.2%	$69,211.69	$155,094.70	77	-9.2%	$69,211.69	$1,758,140.12
15.9%	$71,288.04	$108,466.71	78	23.1%	$71,288.04	$2,092,982.45
2.3%	$73,426.69	$37,534.76	79	-21.7%	$73,426.69	$1,565,378.57
23.5%	$75,629.49	—	80	11.2%	$75,629.49	$1,665,071.48
11.2%	$0	—	81	23.5%	$77,898.37	$1,978,464.91
-21.7%	$0	—	82	2.3%	$80,235.32	$1,943,734.28
23.1%	$0	—	83	15.9%	$82,642.38	$2,170,145.65
-9.2%	$0	—	84	12.2%	$85,121.65	$2,349,781.77
17.6 %	$0	—	85	9.4%	$87,675.30	$2,482,985.95
13.8%	$0	—	86	5.0%	$90,305.56	$2,516,829.69
-9.9%	$0	—	87	16.5%	$93,014.73	$2,839,091.86
5.1%	$0	—	88	12.2%	$95,805.17	$3,089,655.89
7.3%	$0	—	89	9.3%	$98,679.33	$3,278,314.56
11.4%	$0	—	90	-7.1%	$101,639.71	$2,943,914.53
16.2%	$0	—	91	13.6%	$104,688.90	$3,239,598.00
6.8%	$0	—	92	4.9%	$107,829.56	$3,290,508.74
14.3%	$0	—	93	-5.2%	$111,064.45	$3,008,337.84
9.7%	$0	—	94	-13.3%	$114,396.38	$2,493,832.52
26.4%	$0	—	95	-25.1%	$117,828.28	$1,750,052.28

Even though both couples achieve the same average rate of return, the Johnsons run out of money in year fifteen! Why? Because the combination of withdrawals and negative returns early in their retirement years killed off the worker dollars required to sustain their inflation-adjusted lifestyle expenses over time. The lethal combination of retirement withdrawals *and* stock market losses sent their portfolio into a death spiral from which it never recovered. As a result, the Johnsons must endure fifteen years of bare-bones, subsistence-type living, eking out an existence on Social Security alone.

Now, if the Johnsons live for only fifteen years, then the impact of sequence-of-return risk is effectively neutralized. Sure, maybe their children won't receive the inheritance they were hoping for, but the Johnsons won't have to endure fifteen years of poverty. But living a much shorter life is hardly a reasonable (or motivating) solution for mitigating sequence-of-return risk. Given the choice, the Johnsons would much prefer living to a ripe old age *and* never running out of money.

Are you beginning to see the fraught relationship between sequence-of-return risk and longevity risk? The longer you live, the more devastating the consequences should a sequence of negative returns strike a lethal blow to your stock market portfolio in your early retirement years.

WITHDRAWAL RATE RISK

The second sub-risk that gets magnified by longevity risk is withdrawal rate risk. This is the risk of running out of money prior to death as a result of taking unsustainably large annual withdrawals from your retirement accounts.

Prior to the early nineties there was very little science around sustainable withdrawal rates. The prevailing notion held that sustainable withdrawal rates were roughly equal to the average rate of return that could be expected in the stock market over time. For example, if the stock market's historical return was 7 percent, it would follow that you could take 7 percent distributions over a thirty-year retirement without ever depleting your assets.

To understand whether this approach was viable, let's apply that 7 percent withdrawal rate to actual stock market returns from 2000 to 2010.*As you can see, a 7 percent withdrawal rate ($70,000 per year) would have bankrupted your $1 million portfolio 11 years into a 30-year retirement! Retirement poorhouse, here we come!

Well, that was antiquated, outdated pre-1990s thinking, you must be saying to yourself. *Surely Americans in the new*

---

* These are actual returns from the S&P 500 from 2000 to 2010.

Year	Beginning of Year Account Value	Annual Cash Flow	Earnings Rate	End of Year Account Value
2000	$1,000,000	–$70,000	–10.14%	$835,689
2001	$835,698	–$70,000	–13.04%	$665,851
2002	$665,851	–$70,000	–23.37%	$456,601
2003	$456,601	–$70,000	26.38%	$488,586
2004	$488,586	–$70,000	8.99%	$456,217
2005	$456,217	–$70,000	3.00%	$397,803
2006	$397,803	–$70,000	13.62%	$372,450
2007	$372,450	–$70,000	3.53%	$313,126
2008	$313,126	–$70,000	–38.49%	$149,547
2009	$149,547	–$70,000	23.45%	$98,201
2010	$98,201	–$70,000	12.78%	$31,805

millennium have embraced a more enlightened, math-based approach to withdrawal rates. Think again. Consider the study that MetLife did as recently as 2008. They administered a Retirement Income IQ Test to Americans over age fifty and asked a series of questions that included the following: "What percentage of your retirement savings can you withdraw each year while still preserving your principal?" Ready for this? Hang on to your hat! An astounding 43 percent of the respondents said 10 percent! Consider the impact of a 10 percent withdrawal rate on the previous scenario.

Year	Beginning of Year Account Value	Annual Cash Flow	Earnings Rate	End of Year Account Value
2000	$1,000,000	−$100,000	−10.14%	$808,740
2001	$808,740	−$100,000	−13.04%	$616,320
2002	$616,320	−$100,000	−23.37%	$395,656
2003	$395,656	−$100,000	26.38%	$373,650
2004	$373,650	−$100,000	8.99%	$298,252
2005	$298,252	−$100,000	3.00%	$204,199
2006	$204,199	−$100,000	13.62%	$118,391
2007	$118,391	−$100,000	3.53%	$19,040

Based on a 10 percent withdrawal rate ($100,000 per year), you'd run out of money after only 8 years! Without any assets to complement your Social Security, you'd be required to scale back your lifestyle dramatically, move in with the kids, and adopt the scorched-earth rice-and-beans diet advocated by Dave Ramsey. What do you think, could you stomach a steady diet of rice and beans for the next twenty-two years? Probably not quite how you envisioned your golden years.

Have you noticed a trend? Reckless, willy-nilly distributions from your retirement plan can deplete your assets far in advance of your life expectancy. Zeroing in on mathematically acceptable withdrawal rates can help mitigate this risk. We'll discuss how to do so in the next chapter.

LONG-TERM CARE RISK

While outliving one's resources in retirement is frequently listed as retirees' chief preoccupation, not far behind is the concern over a dramatic and unforeseen spending shock. Retirees worry about spending large, unexpected sums of money on out-of-pocket medical costs, housing repairs, family expenses, and marital changes. But the spending shock they're often least prepared for is the one that can be far and away the most financially devastating: long-term care.

Of all the spending shocks that are most likely to send your retirement portfolio spiraling into the abyss, a long-term care event is right at the top of the list. While most shock expenses in retirement can be disruptive, they don't typically clean out the retirement till. Long-term care expenses, however, can force you to burn through a lifetime of savings in just a few short years. This is a spending shock that all too often sends retirement plans into cardiac arrest.

To illustrate the devastating implications of a long-term care event, consider the following conversation I frequently have with my clients:

Me: Mr. Jones, you know I love you, right?

Mr. Jones: Yes, Dave, I know you love me.

Me: I do love you, but you're better off dying than needing long-term care.

Mr. Jones: *[Looking a bit disconcerted.]* Uh, why's that?

Me: Well, at least if you died, your wife would be beneficiary on all your retirement accounts. And while we would miss you terribly, life for her from a financial perspective would continue along relatively unchanged.

[Mr. Jones shifts uncomfortably in his seat, then nods for me to continue.]

Me: If you didn't die, however—let's say you almost died—and ended up needing long-term care, well, that's a different story altogether. Almost all the money set aside for *her* retirement now gets earmarked for the long-term care facility.

She gets to keep one house, one car, a minimum monthly maintenance needs allowance (MMMNA) of about $2,500 per month, and about $128,000 in cash.* So, what was shaping up to be a perfectly rosy retirement for your wife turns into basic, bare-bones, subsistence-type living. And, of course, the same would be true for your wife if she needed long-term care. Then almost all of the retirement savings you were planning on living on get earmarked for the long-term care facility as well.

Sadly, this is a painful scenario that plays out for all too many Americans. Their retirement balances all but dry up due to a devastating and costly long-term care event. And who usually takes the brunt of that long-term care event? It's the community spouse, whose would-be retirement savings are now earmarked for the long-term care facility where their spouse will be living out their remaining years.

So, how does longevity risk compound long-term care risk? It's real simple. The longer you live, the more likely you are to experience a long-term care event. For example, only 1.1 percent of Americans age 65 to 74 are in a nursing home. In other words, the risk of a long-term care event in your

---

* These thresholds can vary from state to state.

first ten years of retirement is statistically negligible. But after 10 more years it's a different story. Once you hit age 85, that number skyrockets all the way up to 15 percent. In short, 15 percent of Americans age 85 and older can no longer perform 2 of 6 activities of daily living.* Between you and your spouse, there's a 28 percent chance that at least one of you will need long-term care by age 85. That's a 28 percent likelihood that you will be forced into spend-down and burn through whatever retirement savings you have left.

Now, if you're both planning on dying at age 85, maybe these long-term care statistics don't seem so menacing. But what if one of you lives longer than that? Statistically speaking, there's a 25 percent chance a 65-year-old male lives to 93 and a 25 percent chance a 65-year-old female lives to 96. And for a 65-year-old couple, there's a 25 percent chance the surviving spouse lives to age 98. What do you think? Could you survive an extra 10 to 15 years in retirement after burning through your savings to pay for your spouse's long-term care? Hardly what you were hoping for! In short, the longer you live, the more likely long-term care will derail your retirement plan. Thanks, longevity risk!

---

* Activities of daily living include eating, bathing, dressing, transferring, continence, and toileting.

INFLATION RISK

Why is money valuable? Because it's scarce! But when you print more of it, it becomes less scarce, and therefore less valuable. That's what we call inflation, and it's a risk that will play an increasingly prominent role in your retirement as our country spirals deeper and deeper into the financial abyss. One of the ways our government hopes to stave off bankruptcy is by printing more money. This is euphemistically referred to as monetization. And as benign as that term sounds, it could exert a massive eroding effect on your purchasing power over the course of your retirement.

To better understand the dangers of inflation, let's review a mathematical principle with which you may already be familiar: the Rule of 72. Here's how it works: divide 72 by your rate of growth, and that tells you how many years it takes to double the value of an asset. For example, if your retirement accounts are growing at 8 percent per year, you could expect them to double in value after 9 years.

When used in reverse, however, this rule can give you a window into the eroding impact of inflation on your retirement savings. Let's use the example of an inflation rate in retirement of only 3 percent. When you divide 72 by 3, you get 24. This means that at 3 percent annual inflation, your purchasing power would be cut in half over a span of only 24 years. What's worse, should the federal government accelerate the pace at which they're printing greenbacks and inflation rise to 6 percent or worse (think 1970s), then your purchasing power would be cut in half in 12 years or sooner.

How does all this tie into longevity risk? By now, the connection should be clear. The longer you live, the more inflation erodes your spending power. But here's the rub: in order to stay ahead of inflation, you have to grow your money. In order to grow your money, you have to take some risk in your retirement portfolio. And the amount of risk required to stay ahead of inflation could expose you, once again, to the insidious effects of sequence-of-return risk. This is a classic catch-22 scenario that, left unaddressed, could send your retirement balances reeling.

IN SUMMARY

Longevity risk is a hard riddle to solve because your retirement investment horizon is a complete unknown. Your retirement could last ten years, thirty-five years, or anywhere in between. This much *is* known, however: the longer you live, the greater the likelihood your retirement gets disrupted by sequence-of-return risk, withdrawal rate risk, long-term care risk, or inflation risk. But don't despair! Throughout this book, I'll show you how a *truly* comprehensive approach to retirement can systematically neutralize *all* the major risks that threaten to derail your retirement plan.

Chapter 3

A TRIP TO MONTE CARLO

For decades Americans managed longevity risk with a loosey-goosey approach to retirement income planning that threw caution to the wind. As I mentioned in the previous chapter, it wasn't unusual for people to withdraw from their retirement portfolios at a rate equal to whatever they felt was the prevailing rate of growth in the stock market at the time. Annual distribution rates between 7 percent and 10 percent were the order of the day. But in 1994, a financial adviser named William Bengen began to push back on the dangerous convention of willy-nilly, haphazard retirement distribution rates. Eyeballing something as critical as retirement withdrawal rates struck him as, well, nonmathematical. To counter this, he employed a computer-based approach to testing withdrawal rates, known as Monte

Carlo simulations. With computer modeling, he ran simulations using historical stock market returns from the previous 70 years. In these simulations he included such variables as length of retirement, stock-bond mix, withdrawal rates, and inflation rates. He wasn't content with 10, 20, or even 1,000 simulations. He wanted his conclusions to be ironclad, so he ran more than 100,000 simulations. And what he discovered curled his hair. Forget 10 percent or even 7 percent distribution rates. Their failure rates were off the charts. Even withdrawal rates as low as 5 percent still had a failure rate as high as 50 percent!

Bengen concluded that a 50-50 stock-bond mix with a 4 percent distribution rate* over a 30-year retirement could be expected to run out of money only 14 percent of the time. While it didn't provide a 100 percent guarantee that you wouldn't outlive your money, it was the first time anyone provided clear definition around sustainable distribution rates in retirement. Retirees were still free to take 7 percent or even 10 percent distributions from their retirement portfolios, but they now understood the risks of doing so. What emerged from Bengen's simulations became

---

* Some retirees who adhere to the Four Percent Rule keep their distributions constant, but the rule does allow them to adjust their distributions to keep up with inflation.

widely known as the Four Percent Rule. This rule soon became the gold standard for sustainable withdrawal rates in retirement.

But within a few decades, cracks began to appear in the veneer of the Four Percent Rule. Economists and retirement experts were questioning how reliable the concept really was. By 2010, these experts concluded that the variables Bengen had used in his Monte Carlo simulations were derived from prevailing economic data that had since grown stale and antiquated. For example, the bond rates he used in his calculations were 5.5 percent, far above the 2 percent rates that are more common in today's economic environment. They further concluded that the long-term stock outlook in the early 1990s was far rosier than it is today.

As a result, retirement experts have downgraded the Four Percent Rule to the Three Percent Rule. In short, to enjoy a reasonably high expectation of not running out of money prior to death, you should never withdraw more than 3 percent of your initial portfolio value in retirement.

While a new, more reliable withdrawal rate standard may speak peace to your soul as it pertains to longevity risk, the Three Percent Rule has four significant shortcomings that could still give you a good case of heartburn.

SHORTCOMING NO. 1: THE PRICE TAG

If the most you can ever withdraw from your retirement portfolio in a given year is 3 percent, it's going to take a staggering amount of capital to fully fund your retirement. For example, assume your annual lifestyle need in retirement is $100,000.* To determine the amount of money you will need to have saved by day one of retirement, divide the desired pretax lifestyle by the maximum sustainable distribution rate, in this case 3 percent. The math looks like this:

$$\frac{\$100,000}{.03}$$

When you divide $100,000 by .03, you find that the total capital required to fund your retirement through life expectancy is $3,333,333.33. In other words, the cost of mitigating longevity risk through stock market investing is well north of $3 million. And while it's relatively easy to

---

* This example assumes the $100,000 lifestyle need is above and beyond what is provided by Social Security, pensions, and other sources of income.

calculate the amount of money you'll need by the time you retire, it's much harder to accumulate it.

Many investors are startled when they realize exactly how much capital is required to fund a retirement plan that adequately addresses longevity risk. Most Americans, studies show, are not on track to accumulate the capital needed to eliminate longevity risk by the time they retire. To bridge their retirement shortfall, they often resort to one or more of the following none-too-appetizing alternatives:

1. **Save more:** This may mean cutting back on your lifestyle during your working years in order to earmark more for your retirement savings.
2. **Spend less:** This option involves lowering expectations for lifestyle spending in retirement. Instead of spending $100,000 per year, for example, you may only be able to spend $80,000.
3. **Work longer:** Pushing off your retirement date does two things: it gives your money more time to grow *and* it shortens the time period over which that money needs to last.
4. **Die sooner:** Does anyone *really* like this option?
5. **Take more risk in the stock market:** By taking more risk with your investments, you *could* grow your money more productively and meet your accumulation goals

by retirement. But taking more risk doesn't guarantee a higher rate of return. More risk means wider swings in your portfolio, which means you could miss your accumulation goal by an even wider margin.

Because of the revised Three Percent Rule, it now takes even more capital to ensure that sequence-of-return risk doesn't sink your retirement ship. It also means you're more likely to have a retirement shortfall today than you ever were under the Four Percent Rule! And if your retirement plan *is* underfunded, these five alternatives are sure to give you a bad case of heartburn!

SHORTCOMING NO. 2: INFLEXIBLE DISTRIBUTIONS

The second shortfall of the Three Percent Rule is that it leaves very little margin for error. In other words, it only really works if you stick to the program. For example, suppose circumstances require you to occasionally stray from the Three Percent Rule. One year you take 5 percent, another year 6 percent, and another year 4 percent. In the very moment you violate your 3 percent threshold, the probability that your money lasts through life expectancy begins to drop. You see, the Three Percent Rule is a jealous master.

For it to work reliably, it has to be obeyed with precision. And that's difficult to do over a 30-year retirement, especially when your retirement savings are liquid, accessible, and clamoring to be spent!

SHORTCOMING NO. 3:
THE NEED FOR DISCIPLINE

The Three Percent Rule requires unflinching discipline when markets are erratic. You've been told to buy low and sell high, but when investors succumb to their emotions during volatile markets, they do just the opposite. They buy high and sell low. As a result, their returns suffer and they fail to harness the growth necessary to make their money last through life expectancy. The Three Percent Rule only really works if you stick with the investment allocation you started with at the beginning of your retirement. If you're constantly moving your stock portfolio to cash every time the market gets jittery, then the complex math that upholds and sustains the Three Percent Rule begins to break down.

In short, the Three Percent Rule requires that you become an emotionless automaton in retirement. Not only do you have to obey the 3 percent withdrawal rate with dogmatic precision, but you have to keep your money fully invested, even when the theater is on fire and everyone is running toward the exit.

SHORTCOMING NO. 4:
THE ILLUSION OF LIQUIDITY

The last shortfall of the Three Percent Rule is its illusion of liquidity. When your retirement distributions are governed by the Three Percent Rule, you aren't nearly as flush as you think. To demonstrate why, let's go back to our $100,000 lifestyle example. To truly eliminate longevity risk, you will have to have accumulated $3,333,333 by day one of retirement. And even though your retirement account is chock-full of cash, practically begging to be spent, you have to remember that every last dollar has been claimed by the Three Percent Rule. All of that money is responsible for generating the income required to pay for your living expenses over the arc of your life expectancy. Not a dollar can be spared. It isn't a buffer account, and it can't be earmarked for those unexpected discretionary expenses that invariably arise.

Because this pile of money *seems* massive, it can easily be mistaken for a spend-at-will discretionary account. Fifty thousand dollars for the roof. Twenty-five thousand for

DISCRETIONARY EXPENSES IN RETIREMENT

Discretionary expenses in retirement break down into two categories:

Shock expenses: As discussed in chapter two, these are unexpected expenses that might include out-of-pocket medical costs, housing repairs, family expenses, and changes in marital status.

Aspirational expenses: These include the costs of travel, gifts to family, hobbies, boat purchases, country club memberships, or other retirement splurges.

some out-of-pocket health care expenses. Ten thousand to take the grandkids to Disney World. Before you know it, you've been seduced by your portfolio's liquidity! As a result of all these seemingly harmless expenditures, the Three Percent Rule—and the high success rate it ensures—goes out the window. You no longer enjoy that high probability of never running out of money in retirement.

Now, there's nothing to prevent you from accumulating an additional pool of money that can meet your discretionary needs in retirement. But that just forces you to accumulate an amount above and beyond the sum required to satisfy the Three Percent Rule.

IN SUMMARY

Adherence to the Three Percent Rule can inject a high degree of predictability into your retirement plan and all but eliminate longevity risk. But it's an awfully expensive way of doing so. It requires accumulating massive amounts of capital that may be beyond the reach of the average investor. What's worse, it requires an unflinching allegiance that leaves very little margin for error. If you think you can amass the required funds and muster the Zen-like discipline necessary to live by the Three Percent Rule, then read no further. But if you're hoping for a less expensive, less angst-inducing way to neutralize longevity risk, I invite you to turn the page.

Chapter 4

GUARANTEED
LIFETIME INCOME

There's a massive X factor when it comes to retirement planning: you simply don't know how long you're going to live. You're trying to solve the most important math equation of your life, and you're missing the most important variable! That's why longevity risk is every retiree's most vexing concern. If you don't make provisions for how long you're *actually* going to live, then you could run out of money before you run out of life. Over the past twenty years, economists and retirement experts have become increasingly convinced that the most efficient way to neutralize longevity risk is to off-load it to the institutions who are in the very business of managing risk: insurance companies.

Ugh! Not insurance companies, you must surely be thinking. *They're the last ones I want poking around in my retirement!* As it turns out, insurance companies are exceptionally adept at managing and mitigating longevity risk. It's what they do. It's their sweet spot. By bringing insurance companies into the picture, you can completely vanquish longevity risk from your retirement plan.

Insurance companies mitigate longevity risk through a technique known as risk pooling. Here's how it works: You give a portion of your investments to the insurance company, who pools it with the assets of thousands of other investors. This enables insurance companies to subsidize the guaranteed income streams of those who live longer lives with the capital of those who live shorter lives. But here's the point: so long as you're alive, that guaranteed income never stops flowing. When it's coupled with other guaranteed streams of income such as Social Security, you can rest assured that your minimum lifestyle requirements are *always* going to be met.*

When you give an insurance company a lump sum of money in exchange for an immediate, guaranteed lifetime stream of income, it's called a *single premium immediate annuity,* or SPIA.

---

* Contractual guarantees are based on the strength and claims-paying ability of the insurance company.

WHAT IS A SINGLE PREMIUM
IMMEDIATE ANNUITY (SPIA)?

Definition: Purchased with a single lump sum, a single premium immediate annuity is a contract between you (the investor) and the insurance company that is designed to create a lifetime stream of supplemental retirement income. Unlike a deferred annuity, an immediate annuity forgoes the accumulation phase and begins paying out guaranteed lifetime income either immediately or within a year of having purchased it. SPIAs are also referred to as income annuities, immediate payment annuities, and immediate annuities.*

Wait, hold the phone, you may be thinking. *Did he just use the most verboten term in all of retirement planning: annuity?* I sure did. And I know what you're thinking: *Isn't Ken Fisher always railing against annuities? Haven't I always been told to be supremely skeptical of them?* There's a lot of misinformation around annuities, but this much I can tell you: if you don't like them, then you almost certainly aren't going to like Social Security or that company pension you

---

* Rachel Cautero, "What Is a Single Premium Immediate Annuity (SPIA)?" Smart-Asset, January 14, 2020, https://smartasset.com/retirement/single-premium-immediate-annuity; "Single Premium Immediate Annuities," Annuity.org, https://www.annuity.org/annuities/immediate/.

may be planning on receiving. Why? Because they're both governed by the exact same risk-pooling principles that govern annuities: those who live shorter lives subsidize the income streams of those who live longer lives.

Once you can get past whatever misgivings you may have about annuities, you'll discover a vast array of positive benefits that stem from receiving a guaranteed stream of lifetime income.

RETIREMENT PREDICTABILITY

The first benefit of guaranteed income for life is the most important and obvious of all. When you guarantee your income for life, you vanquish the biggest bogeyman in retirement planning: longevity risk. You will never run out of money, no matter how long you live. Even if the stock market goes straight down for the entire span of your thirty-year retirement, you will always have food on the table and a roof over your head. Even if you live to age 105, you'll keep getting that check and you'll keep having to find a way to spend it.

ANXIETY-FREE RETIREMENT

When your lifestyle needs are no longer tied to the rise and fall of the stock market, you give yourself permission to enjoy retirement. In fact, according to a study by the *Wall Street Journal,* retirees who have a guaranteed lifetime stream of income are much happier than those who rely on positive returns in the stock market to achieve their retirement goals.*

A LONGER LIFE

If leading a stress-free retirement isn't enough to push you over the hump, consider this: studies have shown that those who have guaranteed lifetime annuities live longer. I know what you're thinking: the type of people who have annuities are the type who have money, and those who have money live longer anyway. While that may be the case, studies further show that all other factors being equal, guaranteed lifetime annuities *still* extend life expectancy. As *Freakonomics'* Stephen Dubner explains, "It's that little extra incentive of the annuity payout that keeps people going."† Jane Austen drove this same point home in *Sense and Sensibility* when she said, "people always live forever when there is an annuity to be paid to them."

---

* Jonathan Clements, "The Secret to a Happier Retirement: Friends, Neighbors and a Fixed Annuity," *Wall Street Journal,* July 27, 2005, https://www.wsj.com/articles/SB112241804795796704.

† "How to Live Longer (Ep. 109): Full Transcript," *Freakonomics* (blog), January 7, 2019, https://freakonomics.com/2013/01/10/how-to-live-longer-full-transcript/.

In short, if that retirement paycheck is guaranteed to arrive so long as you're on this side of the grass, you have a powerful incentive to stay alive! And here's the best part: the longer you live, the greater the return on your investment!

RETIREMENT ON THE CHEAP

Remember one of the biggest shortcomings of the Three Percent Rule? It takes massive quantities of cash to achieve that high probability of never outliving your money. If you need $100,000 per year to meet your basic lifestyle needs,* you will need to have accumulated $3,333,333.33 by day one of retirement, and that doesn't include a discretionary account for shock or aspirational expenses! A guaranteed lifetime annuity, on the other hand, can accomplish the exact same thing, but at a much lower cost.

Consider the following example: You're 65 years old, ready to retire, and you want $100,000 of annual income. You also want an ironclad guarantee that $100,000 income will last as long as you do. So how much money would you have to give to an insurance company in exchange for an

---

* This example assumes the $100,000 lifestyle needed is above and beyond what is provided by Social Security or other sources of retirement income.

immediate, guaranteed lifetime annual income of $100,000? In order to calculate this, you have to determine the going SPIA withdrawal rates for a 65-year old. This number fluctuates based on the insurance company, sex, and the prevailing interest rate environment, but for this example's sake, we'll use 6 percent.

Once you have your guaranteed withdrawal rate, you can apply the same formula we used with the Three Percent Rule, this time substituting in 6 percent. The math goes as follows:

$$\frac{\$100,0000}{.06}$$

When you divide $100,000 by 6 percent, you get $1,666,666.67.* In other words, in order to receive a guaranteed $100,000 income for life, you'd have to give the annuity company $1,666,666.67 on day one of retirement. That's it. End of story. That's half the amount you'd need to accumu-

---

* If in following the Three Percent Rule you choose to adjust your distributions for inflation, you'll need a larger capital outlay to create the equivalent, inflation-adjusted guaranteed lifetime income with the SPIA. Using the lower distribution rate of an inflation-adjusted annuity of 4.5 percent, you would need to contribute $2,222,222.22 to the SPIA at the outset. To read more about inflation-adjusted guaranteed lifetime income, see chapter five.

late by day one of retirement were you to abide by the Three Percent Rule!

Here's the bottom line: a SPIA can give you the same amount of income, *with* an ironclad guarantee and without all the shortcomings of the Three Percent Rule, for half the initial outlay. You can see why more and more financial experts are lauding guaranteed lifetime income annuities as *the* way to permanently remove longevity risk from your retirement portfolio.

HIGH-OCTANE STOCK MARKET INVESTING

Because SPIAs can mitigate longevity risk at half the cost of the Three Percent Rule, you'll have leftover capital to invest in the stock market. And because you're no longer reliant on these liquid investments to meet your basic lifestyle expenses, you can take more risk in your portfolio. *But do I really want to take a lot of risk in my investments when I'm retired?* you might be asking yourself. Remember, just because you're retired doesn't mean it's time to batten down the hatches. Here's why: much of the money you're planning on spending in retirement hasn't even been earned yet! You'll need to harness the power of the stock market to stretch your liquid investments over the full arc of your retirement. This is no time to become a shrinking violet!

Because of the SPIA's ironclad guarantees, you now have the luxury of taking more risk with your liquid investments than you might otherwise take. This in turn increases the likelihood that your stock market assets will last the full length of your retirement. It's the SPIA's permission slip to take more risk in the market that can make the difference between a thrive retirement and a barely-enough-to-survive retirement.

THE DEATH OF SEQUENCE-OF-RETURN RISK AND WITHDRAWAL RATE RISK

When you utilize a SPIA for guaranteed lifetime income, you effectively vanquish two of the deadly retirement risks we discussed in the previous chapter:

Sequence-of-return risk: When you pay for your lifestyle expenses with a SPIA, you are no longer forced to distribute money from your stock market portfolio during down markets. Should the market go down in a given year, you can patiently wait for it to recover before taking additional distributions.

Withdrawal rate risk: When you aren't forced to rely on your stock market portfolio to meet your basic lifestyle needs, you're less likely to prematurely deplete your liquid assets through unduly high distributions. You'll still take distributions, but in much smaller amounts and only for the occasional discretionary expense.

IN SUMMARY

The fact is, guaranteed lifetime income from a single premium immediate annuity can eliminate longevity risk for far less capital than its stock market counterpart. What's more, guaranteed lifetime income gives you permission to feel happier, incentive to live longer, and a larger, more productive investment base from which to pay discretionary expenses that are all but certain to arise during your retirement years. You don't have to love annuities; you just have to love what they can do for you!

Chapter 5

FLIES IN THE OINTMENT

Guaranteed lifetime income in the form of a single premium immediate annuity is clearly adept at eliminating longevity risk in a far less capital-intensive way than the traditional stock market approach. What's more, it confers a long list of psychological, mathematical, and longevity benefits that can smooth out an otherwise rocky road in retirement. If ever there were a simple, effective solution to ensure you never run out of money, it's the SPIA. All this of course begs the question: If the guaranteed-income approach to vanquishing longevity risk is so compelling, why do so few Americans take advantage of it? Over the past decade, retirement savings accounts have nearly doubled from $18 trillion to $32 trillion, but very few of those assets have been used to purchase SPIAs.*

Market studies have shown time and again that America's inherent aversion to annuities boils down to three principal complaints: lack of liquidity, lack of inflation hedge, and the Mack Truck Factor.

LACK OF LIQUIDITY

The first perceived shortcoming of the SPIA is its lack of liquidity. There's no getting around the fact that in order to receive a guaranteed stream of income for life, you have to surrender liquidity on a portion of your retirement assets. You give an insurance company a chunk of your stock market portfolio and they, in turn, give you a stream of income that's guaranteed to last as long as you live. Even though the myriad mathematical, psychological, and health benefits that stem from this exchange have been lauded by study after study, investors can't seem to wrap their brains (or their hearts) around it. Let's face it, there's something reassuring about having a vast supply of cookies sitting in the cookie jar on the kitchen counter that can be accessed at a moment's notice.

---

* "Retirement Assets Total $32.3 Trillion in Fourth Quarter 2019," ICI, https://www.ici .org/research/stats/retirement/ret_19_q4.

LACK OF INFLATION HEDGE

The second objection investors have to the SPIA is its lack of an inflation hedge. When you purchase a SPIA, the insurance company sends you a fixed payment every month for the rest of your life. In their most common form, SPIAs are not designed to keep pace with inflation. This can be a jagged little pill for many investors who are good at math and understand the eroding effects of inflation over time.

Here's an example to illustrate. Let's say you gave an insurance company $500,000 in exchange for a guaranteed lifetime stream of income of $2,500 per month, or $30,000 per year. That $30,000 payment, coupled with your Social Security payments, may be perfectly sufficient to cover your income needs in the here and now. But how about 30 years from now? If the Rule of 72 holds true, then the purchasing power of that $30,000 payment will be more than cut in half by the end of that 30-year time frame. So what started out as a perfectly sound income plan at the beginning of retirement turns into bare-bones, subsistence-type living by the end of it.

To combat this concern, some financial experts simply suggest that you pour even more money into the SPIA in the short term, leaving a buffer for inflation over time. For example, if you need $30,000 to close your income gap today, you might purchase an annuity that gives you $50,000 of income. And while you won't need the full $50,000 today, that inglorious day will soon arrive, thanks to the inexorable effects of inflation. And because you built this inflation buffer into your income plan at the outset, you'll be shielded from its effects later in retirement.

While building an inflation buffer into your income annuity seems like a reasonable approach to combating inflation, it requires *even more* capital in the here and now. This, of course, feeds into the primary objection to SPIAs we discussed earlier: loss of liquidity. In other words, it is possible to solve the inflation conundrum with a SPIA, but only by surrendering an even larger portion of your liquid retirement assets to an insurance company at the outset.

THE MACK TRUCK FACTOR

The last objection to the single premium immediate annuity is what I call the Mack Truck Factor. Here's how it works. Let's say you just handed $500,000 over to an insurance company in exchange for $30,000 of annual guaranteed income for life. You did so in part because you have a Methuselah gene and have every intention of outliving everyone else in the risk pool. You are intent on beating the insurance company at their own game. And then it happens. Two years into retirement you step off the curb and get flattened by a Mack truck. Boom. Game over. Your annual payments come screeching to a halt and the balance of your $500,000 goes to subsidize the guaranteed lifetime income of everyone else in the risk pool. Not only did you lose all that future income, but your heirs got cut out of the equation as well. This possibility, however unlikely, strikes retirees as supremely unfair and discourages a huge number of Americans from ever entering into the transaction.

INSURANCE COMPANIES RESPOND

Insurance companies are not unaware of the perceived deficiencies associated with the SPIA. They understand that, notwithstanding their vast economic and lifestyle benefits, they are embraced by a very small portion of retirees, primarily because of the three aforementioned complaints.

To their credit, insurance companies have adapted and evolved their offerings in an effort to mitigate these objections and appeal to a broader range of retirees. One of the solutions insurance companies have developed to specifically address the shortcomings of the SPIA is an annuity alternative known as a *fixed indexed annuity* (FIA).*

The Liquidity Fix

With a fixed indexed annuity, the insurance company doesn't require that you draw a lifetime income immediately—or ever, for that matter. You can postpone the election of that guaranteed lifetime income until a time of your choosing later in retirement. This provides some measure of liquidity on your assets prior to your electing a guaranteed lifetime income. Once that income option is elected, however, you would have to rely on your non-annuity assets to satisfy your liquidity needs.

The maximum annual distribution during this deferral period is typically 10 percent. Now, you may be thinking, *Wait a minute, 10 percent liquidity isn't the same as full liquidity. I want access to all the cookies all the time!* While it's true you don't have 100 percent liquidity, when you view it within the context of the Three Percent Rule, 10 percent liquidity is practically Mardi Gras. This 10 percent "free out" can go a long way toward assuaging concerns over liquidity.

---

* Some FIA chassis do not include a guaranteed lifetime income benefit. In some cases, this option must be added at the outset of the program and costs around 1 percent of your accumulation value per year.

Inflation Hedge

Prior to electing the guaranteed lifetime income, the FIA's accumulation account grows safely and productively. (The SPIA, in contrast doesn't have an accumulation account, because it doesn't have a deferral period. No deferral period equals no liquidity.) The growth of the accumulation account is linked to the upward movement of a stock market index, such as the S&P 500. Should that stock market index go up in a given year, you participate in that growth, up to a cap.* Should that index ever go down, the insurance company simply credits you a zero. Meaning, you don't ever lose money.

A Couple Caveats

1. While the FIA does allow you to participate in the growth of a stock market index, this growth does not include dividends. This should temper growth expectations because historically dividends account for roughly 30 percent of the annual growth of an index. For example, if the S&P grows 10 percent in a given

---

* This is the most common crediting method. Other methods include participation rates and spreads.

year, 7 percent might be attributed to the actual growth of the underlying stocks, while 3 percent might be attributed to stock dividends.

2. The caps imposed by insurance companies are tied to interest rates. The higher the interest rates, the higher the caps. And given the historically low interest rate environment we've been experiencing of late, those caps aren't exactly at all-time highs.

So, given the combination of dividend exclusion and the current low interest rate environment, you may expect the accumulation account within the FIA to average only a 4 percent rate of return over time.*

Wait, what? you may be thinking. *Why would I take money that could have otherwise been growing at 6 percent to 8 percent in my stock market portfolio and contribute it to an annuity that's only growing at 4 percent? Won't that reduction in rate of return neutralize the benefits that justified the annuity in the first place?* This is where you have to remember your primary motivation for imple-

---

* During the deferral period, some insurance companies offer premium bonuses and interest credit bonuses that apply to the income base from which the guaranteed lifetime income is computed. So even though an index might average only 4 percent per year, the net effect on the income base might be much higher.

menting the FIA. It isn't to achieve stock market returns. It's to lock in a guaranteed lifetime income that keeps pace with inflation. This is where the safe and productive growth of that underlying portfolio becomes so critical. You see, the growth of your guaranteed lifetime income is also linked to the growth of those underlying indexes. Even if those indexes average only 4 percent,* your income is keeping pace with inflation and protecting your purchasing power over the balance of your retirement.

A Death Benefit

To resolve concerns over the Mack Truck Factor, insurance companies stipulate that your beneficiaries receive whatever portion of your FIA's growth account that doesn't get spent during your lifetime. Consider the $500,000 example we cited earlier. Should you get smacked by that Mack truck two years into your retirement, the insurance company will send the unspent portion of the underlying growth account to your beneficiaries. To calculate the total death benefit,

---

* Once your deferral period is over and you elect a guaranteed lifetime income, the growth of that income is linked to the upward movement of a stock market index, but the 1 percent rider charge no longer applies.

simply take the $500,000, add the growth credited to the account, and subtract any payments received prior to your Mack truck encounter.

This death benefit feature can go a long way toward neutralizing the heartburn you feel when contemplating an untimely (and inglorious) demise in your early retirement years. Not only does the FIA allow you to retain liquidity on your assets, but you don't risk disinheriting your heirs should that Methuselah gene never kick in.

Benefit	SPIA	FIA
Guaranteed Lifetime Income	Yes	Yes
Liquidity	No	Yes
Inflation Hedge	No	Yes
Death Benefit	No	Yes

Benefit Comparison: Single Premium Immediate Annuity vs. Fixed Indexed Annuity

The above chart highlights the traditional deficiencies of the single premium immediate annuity approach and explains why fixed indexed annuities are gaining currency among retirees.

A CRACK IN THE FIA FACADE?

On the surface, the fixed indexed annuity seems ideally suited to meet your guaranteed lifetime income needs without the heartburn of the traditional SPIA approach. The 10 percent annual free withdrawal gives you more than enough flexibility to assuage concerns over liquidity. And thanks to the annuity's index features, that stream of income can keep pace with inflation over time. Finally, the death benefit does a nice job of alleviating the angst you feel at the prospect of dying early and having a massive retirement asset disappear from your balance sheet. With the FIA, insurance companies appear to have aligned the stars. What could possibly go wrong?

The Dangers of Tax Rate Risk

Although the traditional use of the FIA addresses longevity risk in a satisfying way, it largely ignores the other huge retirement risk: tax rate risk. During my more than twenty years in the financial services industry, I've made a troubling observation: 95 percent of all retirement accounts in the United States are situated within the tax-deferred bucket. These include qualified plans such as IRAs, 401(k)s, 403(b)s, and 457 plans. Remember, when you contribute money to these accounts, it's like going into a business partnership with the IRS, and every year, they get to vote on what percentage of your profits they get to keep. Doesn't sound like a very good business partnership, huh? So, you could have $1 million in your IRA, but unless you can accurately predict what tax rates are going to be when you take the money out, you really don't know how much money you have. And it's hard to plan for retirement if you don't know how much you have.

Given this backdrop, let's examine the single greatest shortcoming in the way the FIA is traditionally implemented. Retirees who utilize the FIA for guaranteed lifetime income do so almost exclusively within the tax-deferred bucket. They roll a portion of their tax-deferred retirement assets into an FIA and, after a period of deferral, elect their guaranteed lifetime stream of income. But they often do so without any thought for the cascade of unintended tax consequences that follow.

It's important to note that once you elect a guaranteed lifetime stream of income from the FIA within the tax-deferred bucket, it will be taxed at ordinary income rates for the rest of your life. That's all well and good should tax rates stay level for the balance of your retirement. But if taxes rise to the level necessary to keep our country from going bankrupt, you'll keep much less of that guaranteed income stream than you ever thought possible.

For example, let's assume you have a guaranteed monthly income that starts out at $4,000. Let's also assume your effective tax rate is 20 percent.* In this scenario, your after-tax monthly income is $3,200. It's not the end of the world. In fact, that may be precisely what your income plan requires. But what if tax rates double over time, as predicted by former comptroller general of the federal government David Walker? At 40 percent effective tax rates, your net monthly income drops to only $2,400. Now you have an $800 hole in your monthly income. But that's only the beginning of your problems. Because the lifetime income from the FIA is designed to grow over time, that hole in your income grows right along with it.

How will you plug that ever-expanding hole in your guaranteed income stream? By taking more money out of your stock market portfolio. Not only will you lose that money, but you'll lose what it could have earned for you had you been able to keep it and invest it over the balance of your retirement. As a result, you'll run out of liquid capital much sooner than you ever thought possible.

---

* This includes both state and federal tax.

What's worse, if you're forced to spend down your stock market portfolio to compensate for the hole in your retirement income, you invite that old nemesis sequence-of-return risk back into your retirement picture. If higher taxes force you to withdraw money from your stock market portfolio during a down year, then your retirement assets take a double hit. This means you'll have even less money to address those discretionary needs later in retirement.

In short, even though the pretax amount you're receiving from the insurance company is guaranteed, the after-tax amount is not. That part is subject to the constantly growing capital needs of a revenue-hungry federal government. Such are the dangers of electing a guaranteed lifetime stream of income from your tax-deferred bucket!

Social Security Taxation

The second significant disadvantage of drawing lifetime income from your tax-deferred bucket is Social Security taxation. It's important you recognize that the IRS keeps tabs on something called *provisional income*.

That's the income they track to determine if they're going to tax your Social Security. Any 1099s that come out of your taxable bucket count as provisional income, as do any distributions from your tax-deferred bucket. To make mat-

WHAT IS PROVISIONAL INCOME?

The IRS keeps track of provisional income to determine the portion of your Social Security that gets taxed. The following is a list of common sources of provisional income:

1. Half of your Social Security income
2. Distributions from your tax-deferred bucket (IRAs, 401(k)s, etc.)
3. 1099s from your taxable bucket investments
4. Employment income
5. Rental income
6. Municipal bond interest

The IRS calculates your provisional income, and based on that total and your tax filing status, it determines the portion of your Social Security that will be taxed. The provisional income thresholds are outlined below.

JOINT PROVISIONAL INCOME FOR MARRIED COUPLES	
Provisional Income	Percent of Social Security Subject to Tax
Under $32,000	0%
$32,000 to $44,000	Up to 50%
Over $44,000	Up to 85%

INDIVIDUAL PROVISIONAL INCOME FOR SINGLE PEOPLE	
Provisional Income	Percent of Social Security Subject to Tax
Under $25,000	0%
$25,000 to $34,000	Up to 50%
Over $34,000	Up to 85%

ters worse, half of your Social Security *also* counts as provisional income. The IRS adds all this provisional income up, and if it totals more than $34,000 for a single person or more than $44,000 for a married couple, then up to 85 percent of your Social Security can become taxable at your highest marginal tax bracket!

It's important to recognize that any guaranteed lifetime income drawn from the tax-deferred bucket is considered provisional income by the IRS. So not only could you lose a portion of your guaranteed income to rising taxes, but you could unwittingly forfeit a portion of your Social Security as well! Having done thousands of these calculations over the years, I can tell you it isn't unusual to pay anywhere from $3,000 to $6,000 in Social Security taxation due to high levels of provisional income. But that's only the beginning of your problems. Should tax rates double over time, your Social Security tax bill doubles right along with it! And how will you plug that ever-expanding hole in your Social Security? You guessed it! By taking even larger distributions from your stock market portfolio!

A Double Whammy

Consider the impact on your investment portfolio were you required to compensate for holes in your guaranteed income *and* your Social Security due to rising taxes. I've looked at this from every possible angle and here's the cold, hard truth: these additional distributions could force you to spend down your stock market portfolio twelve to fifteen years faster than you otherwise planned. And that's assuming you didn't succumb to sequence-of-return risk along the way!

IN SUMMARY

Traditionally, investors have steered clear of guaranteed lifetime income annuities because of concerns over lack of:

- liquidity
- inflation hedge
- death benefit feature

The insurance industry has done an admirable job creating a tool that addresses these concerns in a way that satisfies the average consumer. By building a 10 percent penalty-free withdrawal into the FIA, they assuage concerns over lack of liquidity. Furthermore, because the guaranteed income stream is linked to the growth of a stock market index, you have ample opportunity to keep pace with inflation. Lastly, the FIA's death benefit feature gives you the luxury of dying without disinheriting your beneficiaries.

With the FIA, insurance companies *have* addressed longevity risk in a satisfactory way. But they've largely ignored the tax implications of drawing lifetime income from the tax-deferred bucket in a rising tax rate environment. And by ignoring these unintended consequences, they neutralize much of the safety and security that justified the purchase of the fixed indexed annuity in the first place. In the next chapter, I'll show how a few insurance companies have created provisions within their FIAs that allow you to neutralize these deficiencies in order to shield you from both longevity risk *and* tax rate risk in a way that will restore peace and predictability to your retirement plan.

Chapter 6

ALIGNING THE STARS

To combat the effects of higher taxes and Social Security taxation, most insurance companies allow investors to convert their fixed indexed annuity to a Roth IRA *prior* to electing their guaranteed lifetime income. In theory, this solves two problems. First, a tax-free guaranteed lifetime annuity is immune to tax rate risk. Never at any point would you have to spend down your stock market assets to compensate for rising tax rates. Second, because distributions from Roth IRAs do not count as provisional income, you are perfectly positioned to receive your Social Security 100 percent tax-free.

But sadly, not all is as rosy as it seems. While all insurance companies allow for a Roth conversion within the FIA itself, the vast majority of these companies require that the conversion be undertaken *all in one year*.

To illustrate the disastrous consequences of this requirement, consider the following example. Let's assume you had a $1 million FIA held within your IRA. Let's also assume you needed $100,000 of pretax income to meet your lifestyle needs in retirement. You recognize the implications of tax rate risk and Social Security taxation and want to shift your money to tax-free. The insurance company gives you permission to convert your FIA to a Roth IRA, so long as you convert the full $1 million *in one year*.

To understand how this could impact you, I'd like you to think back to that long, skinny cylinder from your high school chemistry class. That's right, a graduated cylinder. Well, the tax system in our country works exactly like that graduated cylinder. When you distribute money from your IRA, either to spend or to convert to a Roth IRA, that income goes into your tax cylinder and flows all the way down to the bottom. Some of your money gets taxed at 10 percent, some at 12 percent, some at 22, 24, 32, 35, and 37 percent. You can see these tax cylinders in the exhibit below.*

If you converted your entire $1 million IRA in one year, all of that income would flow into your tax cylinder and land

---

* At the time of this writing, 2021 tax brackets are not yet available.

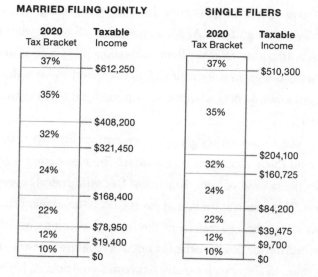

right on top of your lifestyle income. That means your total gross income for the year would be $1.1 million! When you account for both state and federal tax, that could push your effective tax rate as high as 40 percent. So what, exactly, have you done? In an effort to avoid a doubling of tax rates over time, you doubled your tax rates in the short term!

A BETTER WAY

Some forward-thinking insurance companies (only four at the time of this writing) have provisions that allow for something that's altogether revolutionary in the world of tax-free retirement planning. Instead of requiring you to convert your entire IRA in one year, they allow for what I call a *piecemeal internal Roth conversion* (PIRC). In other words, they grant you the flexibility of converting your IRA in any amount, over whatever time period you deem appropriate.

What's more, they give you two options for paying the tax on those piecemeal conversions. The first option is to pay the tax out of your 10 percent free withdrawals every year. This would allow you to pay the tax without incurring any surrender charges from the insurance company. The second option is to pay the tax out of a separate investment account in either your taxable or tax-deferred bucket. If you have enough money in your taxable bucket to pay the tax, this is by far the superior approach. You preserve all of the assets in your most tax-efficient bucket (tax-free) and spend down the assets in your least tax-efficient bucket (taxable) along the way. This approach allows you to preserve 100 percent of the tax-free, inflation-adjusted guaranteed lifetime income you'll eventually draw from your FIA. Talk about aligning your tax-free stars!

Now that we know that the PIRC is an option, consider the following example. Let's assume you had that same $1 million FIA within your IRA along with the $100,000 pretax lifestyle need from the previous example. Let's also assume you've postponed Social Security until after the Roth conversion period is over. We can further assume that given your financial situation, you want to convert the entire annuity to a Roth IRA before the 2018 tax cuts expire in 2026 and tax rates go up. Finally, we'll assume that the underlying FIA accumulation account averages 3 percent net of fees over the Roth conversion period.

Given all this information, you'd need to convert roughly $218,000 per year from the IRA inside your fixed indexed annuity to a Roth IRA over that five-year period. There are two major benefits of following this course. First, given your ability to spread the taxes out over five years, you would pay taxes on those conversions primarily in the 22 percent and 24 percent tax brackets. This would save you massive amounts of taxes over the all-in-one-year Roth conversion required by most annuity companies. Second, by completing the conversion within that five-year time frame, you'll finish paying those taxes before the tax sale ends in 2026. Once 2026 rolls around, that 22 percent tax bracket becomes 25 percent, and the 24 percent tax bracket becomes 28 percent. And as we move past 2026 to 2028, 2030, and beyond, tax rates will have to rise even higher to keep our country out of bankruptcy.

IN SUMMARY

If punitive, all-in-one-year Roth conversion features are any indication, most insurance companies have put very little thought into the implications of tax rate risk. By requiring that Roth conversions be executed all in one year, they exacerbate the tax consequences the conversion was calculated to avoid. Fortunately, a few proactive insurance companies recognize what's at stake and have allowed for piecemeal internal Roth conversions. This allows you to spread your tax liability over multiple years in an effort to maximize your after-tax income in retirement. By paying less tax during your conversion period, you can maximize your tax-free income *and* receive your Social Security 100 percent tax-free. As a result, you won't be forced to spend down your stock market portfolio to compensate for all that additional taxation. That means you'll have much more money to pay for discretionary expenses later in retirement.

Chapter 7

SURVIVING THE ROTH
CONVERSION GAUNTLET

One of the constraints of the piecemeal internal Roth conversion of the fixed indexed annuity is that you won't be able to draw your guaranteed lifetime income until your conversion is complete. That could take anywhere from one to ten years, depending on the size of your IRA, and the level of annual taxation you feel comfortable paying. Given this waiting period, a question naturally arises: How will you pay for your lifestyle and other cash flow expenses in the meantime?

This is where the non-annuity portion of your retirement portfolio plays a critical role. Because it takes much less capital to neutralize longevity risk through an FIA than it does through the Three Percent Rule, you'll still have money left in your stock market portfolio. A portion of these remaining assets must be earmarked for three critical cash flow needs during the Roth conversion period.

CASH FLOW NEED NO. 1: YOUR LIFESTYLE

One of your largest cash flow needs during the Roth conversion period is your lifestyle expenses. For this reason, it's best to complete your conversion in as short a period as makes financial sense. The sooner you complete your Roth conversion, the sooner you can elect your guaranteed lifetime income, and the less money you'll have to spend on your lifestyle in the meantime. Furthermore, shorter conversion periods increase the likelihood you'll finish paying taxes on those conversions before tax rates go up for good.

CASH FLOW NEED NO. 2: YOUR LIFE INSURANCE RETIREMENT PLAN

In chapter two, we discussed how long-term care can force you to burn through a lifetime of savings in just a few short years. We also discussed the devastating effects a long-term care event can have on the community spouse. This is where a *life insurance retirement plan* (LIRP) can play an important role in mitigating this insidious risk.

THE THREE PRIMARY BENEFITS
OF THE LIRP IN RETIREMENT

1. **Death benefit:** One of the primary purposes of the LIRP is to provide a death benefit. This can be especially useful in replacing lost income from Social Security, a pension, or a guaranteed lifetime income stream from an annuity following the death of a spouse.

2. **Long-term care:** Many LIRP companies will give you your death benefit in advance of your death for the purpose of paying for long-term care. This can spare the community spouse from having to spend down the majority of their retirement assets to pay the devastating costs of long-term care for their spouse. If forced into spend-down, the community spouse gets to keep one house, one car, a minimum monthly maintenance needs allowance (MMMNA) of about $2,500 per month, and about $128,000 in cash. The IRS could even force the community spouse to surrender a portion of their guaranteed lifetime income annuity to pay for their spouse's long-term care!

3. **Tax-free growth:** The IRS allows the money within the growth account of the LIRP to accumulate tax-free and be distributed tax-free. Because this money is growing in a safe and productive environment, it becomes an ideal place from which to draw money for aspirational or shock expenses later in retirement, especially following a down year in the stock market. This allows your stock portfolio to recover, sparing you from the pernicious effects of sequence-of-return risk.

An LIRP is a life insurance policy specifically designed to build cash within the policy's growth account. It does this by turning the traditional approach to life insurance on its ear. Conventional wisdom says that when you buy life insurance, you should purchase as much death benefit as you can for as little money as possible. With an LIRP, you purchase as little death benefit as is required by the IRS and stuff as much money into it as the IRS allows. When structured in this way, the LIRP is ideally suited to mitigate a number of risks that threaten to derail your retirement plan, including the risk of a long-term care event.

The LIRP has a number of critical features that make it a compelling fixture in your tax-free income strategy. First, money within its accumulation account grows tax-deferred and can be distributed tax-free. Second, the LIRP's death benefit can be accessed in advance of your death for the purpose of paying for long-term care. And should you die peacefully in your sleep thirty years from now, never having needed long-term care, someone's still getting a tax-free death benefit.

In most cases, the LIRP can be fully funded over the same time period required to complete the Roth conversion of your FIA. The cash flow required to fund your LIRP will also be funded from the non-annuity portion of your retirement portfolio.

CASH FLOW NEED NO. 3: TAXES

During the Roth conversion period you'll need to set aside liquid capital to pay for taxes. Now, paying taxes on your retirement accounts prior to when the IRS absolutely requires it may go against your most natural impulses, so I give you permission to *not* enjoy it. But when given the choice between paying taxes at historically low rates and postponing the payment of those taxes to a later date when the rates are likely to be much higher, you're definitely better off paying them today. The money required to pay these taxes will also come from the non-annuity portion of your retirement savings.

ONCE AGAIN, SEQUENCE-OF-RETURN RISK

The money earmarked for lifestyle expenses, LIRP contributions, and taxes during the Roth conversion period must be invested in such a way that it stays ahead of inflation while shielding you from sequence-of-return risk. For that reason, these funds can't be invested in a traditional stock market allocation. Should the stock market take a spill during the Roth conversion period, you would be forced to liquidate your retirement accounts while they're down. This could strike a devastating blow to your liquid assets in those critical early years of retirement. Even though you'd still receive that guaranteed stream of income at the end of your Roth conversion period, you'd have fewer assets with which to pay those discretionary expenses later in retirement.

TIME-SEGMENTED INVESTING DURING THE ROTH CONVERSION PERIOD

One way to protect the assets earmarked for your cash flow needs during the Roth conversion period is through a strategy known as time-segmented investing. Here's how it works: Assume you want to convert your annuity to a Roth IRA over a ten-year time frame.* You would allocate the cash flow required to pay for your lifestyle, LIRP contributions, and taxes during that ten-year period to a series of portfolios whose time horizons mature at a point in time when you need the money. Any assets not required to meet your cash flow needs during this conversion period would be allocated to a post–Roth conversion portfolio primarily comprising aggressive-growth stocks.

---

* A ten-year Roth conversion time frame is not ideal because you run the risk of much higher taxes beyond 2026. However, I use the ten-year example here to fully illustrate the benefits of time-segmented investing.

Time-segmented investing within the framework of this strategy requires six separate accounts that match the following time horizons:

- Cash account (year 1): less than 1 percent return
- Portfolio 1 (years 2–3): 2.5 percent return
- Portfolio 2 (years 4–5): 3.5 percent return
- Portfolio 3 (years 6–7): 4 percent return
- Portfolio 4 (years 8–10): 4.5 percent return
- Portfolio 5 (post–Roth conversion) 6.5 percent return*

Let's take a moment to expand upon these portfolios.

Cash: This is money earmarked for your lifestyle expenses in year one. You can't afford to expose these dollars to any amount of risk. They must be available when your liquidity needs arise. From a practical perspective, it makes sense to deposit this money into a checking, savings, or money market account. This would allow you to automate the payment of your bills without exposure to the ebb and flow of an investment account.

---

* These returns are subject to prevailing interest rate environments and do not include investment fees.

Portfolios 1 through 4: The money allocated to cash flow needs during years two through ten of the Roth conversion period are subdivided into portfolios that segment risk according to four separate time horizons. Remember, we aren't after explosive stock market returns in these portfolios—we simply want to keep pace with inflation and eliminate sequence-of-return risk. Each separate portfolio invests in bonds that have durations that correspond to the time horizon of that segment. For example, portfolios that wouldn't have to be accessed until year seven would include bond offerings with longer durations, and slightly more risk, than portfolios that need to be accessed in year two. In short, each portfolio is uniquely tailored to meet the risk sensitivity of its respective time segment within the ten-year Roth conversion period.

The amount allocated to Portfolios 1 through 4 at the beginning of your retirement would be the net present value required to accumulate the appropriate amount of money to pay for those cash flow needs by the time horizon indicated. For example, if we anticipate that the cash flow needed in year eight will grow at 4.5 percent between now and then, we can allocate less money to Portfolio 4 at the beginning of the Roth conversion period, and allow it to grow to the required sum by the time we need to access it. This allows us to allocate as little money as possible to these lower-return portfolios.

Portfolio 5, high-octane investing: The portion of your liquid assets not earmarked for cash flow needs during the Roth conversion period is allocated to Portfolio 5, a much higher-octane, growth-oriented investment portfolio. In the preceding Roth conversion example, any portion of your portfolio not earmarked for your cash flow needs during that ten-year period would, by default, spill over into Portfolio 5.

There are three reasons why the post–Roth conversion dollars allocated to Portfolio 5 can be invested in such an aggressive fashion. First, because you won't need liquidity on these dollars during the Roth conversion period, you have the luxury of taking more risk. Should the market go down during the conversion period, you'll have time to let these assets recover. Second, once the Roth conversion period is over and your basic lifestyle expenses are covered by your Social Security and your guaranteed lifetime income, you won't have to take distributions during a down market to pay for discretionary needs. Say good-bye to sequence-of-return risk! Lastly, by investing the money in Portfolio 5 more aggressively, you increase the likelihood it will last your whole retirement.

IN SUMMARY

Because you won't have access to your guaranteed lifetime income until the end of your Roth conversion period, you need a reliable pool of funds from which to pay for your lifestyle expenses, LIRP contributions, and taxes. Given the dangers of sequence-of-return risk during these early years of retirement, you can't risk growing these funds in the stock market. To neutralize this risk during the Roth conversion period, it makes more sense to grow those dollars in time-segmented, risk-adjusted portfolios that grow safely and productively. This frees up the balance of your non-annuity portfolio to be invested in high-octane investments that can grow much more productively, increasing the likelihood they'll survive as long as you do.

Chapter 8

PUTTING IT ALL TOGETHER

So far, we've identified two massive risks that threaten to derail even the most thoughtful and intentional retirement plans. Rising taxes can dramatically reduce your after-tax spendable cash flow in retirement, while living too long enhances and magnifies a subset of risks that can land you in the poorhouse decades before your anticipated life expectancy. We've also identified the pros and cons of the two traditional approaches to mitigating longevity risk. Finally, we laid out a revolutionary strategy that, when implemented properly, can purge tax rate risk *and* longevity risk from your retirement portfolio.

Before demonstrating how this comprehensive strategy might work in a real-life scenario, it's important that we review the tax-free retirement approach discussed in *The*

Power of Zero. We begin by identifying the three basic types of accounts within which to accumulate retirement savings. I refer to these three accounts as buckets of money. It's critical to recognize that in a rising-tax-rate environment, there is an ideal amount of money to have in each of these buckets.

THE TAXABLE BUCKET

The first bucket of money is called the *taxable bucket.* Every year as the money within this bucket grows, you get to pay a tax. This bucket can include investments such as CDs, money markets, stocks, bonds, mutual funds, etc. These types of investments are useful because they're generally very liquid and instantly accessible without penalties. For these reasons, they make for great emergency funds. Retirement experts generally agree that you should have no more than six months of basic living expenses in these types of accounts.

THE TAX-DEFERRED BUCKET

The second bucket of money is called the *tax-deferred bucket.* Common examples include 401(k)s, IRAs, 403(b)s, and 457 plans. In these accounts, you contribute pretax dollars, your money grows tax-deferred, and you pay tax upon distribution. These types of accounts should be used only in carefully prescribed ways, especially given the almost certainty of higher taxes in the future.

Because you'll still have the standard deduction available to you in retirement, it's OK to have *some* money in these types of accounts. The standard deduction allows you to realize income from any number of sources, including tax-deferred retirement plans, up to a certain threshold without paying any taxes at all. For example, if you retired today, absent any other deductions, you'd still have a standard deduction of $24,800.* That means you could withdraw up to $24,800 from your tax-deferred retirement accounts completely tax-free. Keep in mind, however, that any distributions from this bucket count as provisional income and could cause up to 85 percent of your Social Security to be taxed at your highest marginal tax bracket. So, just because you *can* withdraw $24,800 from your tax-deferred bucket doesn't mean that you *should*.

In short, we want balances in this bucket to be low enough that *required minimum distributions* (RMDs) are equal to or less than our standard deduction in retirement, as well as low enough that those RMDs don't cause Social

---

* This amount is $12,400 for a single filer. These deductions increase by $1,300 for single people and $2,600 for a married couple once you reach age 65. The 2021 standard deduction amount is not available at the time of this writing.

Security taxation. To calculate the ideal balance in your tax-deferred bucket, check out my magic-number calculator at davidmcknight.com.

THE TAX-FREE BUCKET

In the *tax-free bucket*, you make contributions with dollars that have already been taxed. Once those dollars are safely ensconced within the tax-free bucket, they can be distributed tax-free, even if tax rates rise dramatically over time. Now, there are a variety of investments that masquerade as tax-free, but to be truly tax-free an investment has to qualify in two different ways. First, it has to *be* free from federal, state, and capital gain taxes. Second, distributions from a truly tax-free investment cannot count as provisional income. They cannot count against the thresholds that cause Social Security taxation. Tax-free investments that satisfy both criteria include Roth IRAs, Roth 401(k)s, Roth conversions, and LIRPs.

SHIFTING SURPLUS TO TAX-FREE

Now that we've established the ideal balances in your taxable and tax-deferred buckets, you're ready to maneuver your way toward the 0 percent tax bracket. Anything above and beyond the ideal balances in the taxable and tax-deferred buckets should be systematically repositioned to tax-free. But you don't want to do it all at once! The key is to shift money slowly enough that you don't rise into a tax bracket that gives you heartburn, but quickly enough that you get all the heavy lifting done before tax rates go up for good. As of 2021, that gives you only five years to get your hard-earned retirement savings repositioned to tax-free!

Unlocking the 0 Percent Tax Bracket

To help you understand the importance of achieving the proper balance in each of your three buckets, consider the following analogy. If you look at a key, you'll notice that its teeth rise and fall in a series of ridges and valleys. In order for that key to unlock the tumblers in a lock, those ridges must be precisely the right height and those valleys precisely the right depth. And so it goes with the balances within your three buckets. In order to unlock the 0 percent tax bracket, each of those balances must be at precisely the right level.

For example, if the balances in your tax-deferred bucket are too high, required minimum distributions at age seventy-two can overwhelm your standard deduction and put you at risk of higher taxes. What's more, your high levels of provisional income could cause your Social Security to be taxed, forcing you to spend down your stock market portfolio to compensate. Through a proactive shifting strategy, however, you can position the ideal amount of assets in each of your buckets and permanently eliminate tax rate risk from your retirement equation.

CASE STUDY: MITIGATING TAX RATE RISK *AND* LONGEVITY RISK

Now that we've reviewed how to insulate your retirement plan from higher taxes, I'll show you a step-by-step approach to eliminating tax rate risk *and* longevity risk. This is a good time to remind you that this process will add a bit of complexity to your retirement plan in the short term. Just remember that when things do veer into the complex, I'll be at your side explaining and clarifying every step along the way!

To help illustrate this step-by-step strategy, we'll discuss the case of Mike and Julie Smith. Before I proceed with the case study, it is important to note that the Smiths' financial scenario is likely very different from yours. In fact, there may be massive disparities between their retirement picture and your own. Keep in mind, however, that there will be much in this example that *does* pertain to you, so watch for how these principles might apply to your specific situation.

Mike and Julie Smith just retired at age sixty. Their financial profile is as follows:

GENERAL INFORMATION

Mike's age: 60
Julia's age: 60
Annual after-tax lifestyle requirement: $80,000
Anticipated inflation rate: 3 percent

ASSETS

Taxable Bucket

Mutual funds: $400,000

Tax-Deferred Bucket

Mike's IRA $750,000
Julie's IRA $750,000

Tax-Free Bucket

$0

Social Security

Combined $40,000 at age 65*

Insurance

No life insurance
No long-term care insurance

---

* Social Security benefits are expressed in today's dollars. For example, assume you're 60 and your Social Security statement says you'll collect $2,500 per month at age 67. By the time you draw your Social Security benefit at age 67, that $2,500 will have been adjusted for inflation, resulting in a higher benefit.

CHILDREN

Three adult children, ages 35, 33, and 30.

MISCELLANEOUS DATA

Mike and Julie believe taxes will rise dramatically over time and want to execute their asset-shifting program before the current tax cuts expire in 2026.

HOW LONG WILL YOU LIVE?

One of the key details you'll need when formulating your retirement plan is a clear idea of how long you are going to live. This critical data can inform a number of key decisions in your retirement plan:

Social Security: When should you draw Social Security? This is an easier decision to make once you determine how long you're going to live. The longer you live, the more likely you are to reach your Social Security break-even age. This is the age at which you'd come out ahead by postponing Social Security rather than taking it early.

Retirement date: Establishing the ideal retirement date is much easier once you know your life expectancy. The last thing you want is to work all the way until age seventy, collect your gold watch, only to die at age seventy-one!

Income annuity owner: In a scenario in which both you and your spouse have substantial IRAs, you're faced with an important question: Whose IRA do you use to guarantee the lifetime income? If you know which spouse will live longer, then the guaranteed lifetime income should be drawn from that spouse's IRA. By choosing to receive the income over the longer of the two spouses' lives, you can generally maximize your cumulative distributions over time.

ODDSMAKERS IN VEGAS

Knowing how long you're going to live is a critical variable in retirement planning, but is there an accurate way to determine the answer? Turns out there is a rather scientific way of doing so. As an important first step in vanquishing both tax rate risk and longevity risk, I typically suggest you go through the underwriting process for the LIRP. This may sound a bit macabre, but life insurance underwriters are in the business of predicting how long you're going to live. That's their whole job! They're like oddsmakers in Vegas. When they give you a life insurance rating they are, in essence, predicting your life expectancy. And they're willing to put their money where their mouth is in the form of a death benefit. Once you know how long you and your spouse are expected to live, you can make the aforementioned retirement decisions with a much higher degree of confidence.

A Step-by-Step Plan to Mitigate Tax Rate Risk
and Longevity Risk

Step 1: Qualify for the LIRP

The first step in the Smiths' retirement planning process is to qualify for the LIRP. As part of the underwriting process, Mike and Julie will meet with a traveling nurse, answer a series of health questions, and provide blood and urine samples. They'll also have to sign a HIPAA waiver giving the underwriter full access to their medical records. The underwriter gathers this information, evaluates it, and then comes back with a prediction as to how long Mike and Julie are going to live. The underwriter expresses this prediction in the form of a life insurance rating. It's important to note that you can receive as many as thirty different life insurance ratings. If you get the top one, that means you walk on water; you're going to live forever. If you get the bottom one, they basically have to hold out a mirror to see if you fog it. The closer Mike and Julie are to that top rating, the more it makes sense to include the LIRP as part of their plan to mitigate tax rate risk and longevity risk.

Before beginning their LIRP qualification process, Mike and Julie must determine the size of their respective death benefits. If they're using the LIRP to protect against a long-term care event, then they should each have *at least* $400,000 of death benefit. Here's why: should one of them end up needing long-term care, they'll receive 25 percent of that death benefit every year for four years. That's $100,000 per year over that four-year time frame.* When coupled with their Social Security, that should be more than enough to cover their monthly expenses over the arc of a typical long-term care stay. And should they die peacefully in their sleep thirty years from now, never having needed long-term care, their beneficiaries will receive a tax-free death benefit. This approach eliminates the heartburn associated with the traditional use-it-or-lose-it approach to long-term care insurance.

For the purpose of this case study, let's assume that Julie received the top rating and Mike received the third-best rating. Given this result, it *would* make sense for both Mike and Julie to implement their respective LIRPs.

Step 2: Implement the LIRP

Now that Mike and Julie are approved, their next step is to implement their LIRPs. This is accomplished by submitting the first-year contributions for both policies to the insurance company. In Mike and Julie's case, this funding would

---

* This amount will be discounted by the insurance company based upon your attained age when you receive the benefit. The younger your age, the greater the discount.

come directly from their IRAs. Given their goal of completing their asset-shifting plan by 2026, and assuming death benefits of $400,000 each, they would need to shift a total of $45,000 per year for 5 years. We'll talk about how to pay the tax on that $45,000 annual IRA distribution shortly.

The implementation of the LIRPs goes a long way toward removing long-term care risk from the Smiths' retirement picture. What's more, they'll build a tax-free pool of money from which to pay aspirational and shock expenses later in retirement.

Step 3: Calculate the Income Gap

Our next step is to determine Mike and Julie's retirement income gap. This will help determine what portion of their IRAs should be contributed to their fixed indexed annuity for the purpose of creating a guaranteed stream of lifetime income.

To determine Mike and Julie's retirement income gap, we add up their anticipated sources of guaranteed income* in today's dollars, and then subtract that total from their total after-tax income requirement in today's dollars. This after-tax income requirement should also include a small

---

* In Mike and Julie's case, this only includes Social Security. If they had a pension, this would also be included.

THE TIMING OF LIRP DISTRIBUTIONS

There are two caveats when it comes to the timing of LIRP distributions. First, LIRPs need time to marinate. You generally don't want to take distributions from the LIRP until after the tenth policy year. The LIRP's growth account needs a full ten years to build a head of steam. Second, given the safe and productive nature of the LIRP's growth account, you're better off taking distributions when your stock market portfolio is down. Even though sequence-of-return risk isn't as dangerous after the first ten years of retirement, this approach is likely to extend the life of your stock market investments.

buffer amount for minor contingencies throughout the year. In the Smiths' case, that calculation is as follows:

After-tax lifestyle requirement	$80,000 (in today's dollars)
Social Security	$40,000 (in today's dollars)
	$40,000 (income gap)

Once we know Mike and Julie's income gap, we have one additional step. Because their guaranteed lifetime income won't begin until the Roth conversion period is over, we have to inflate their income gap over the intervening years.

When we inflate that $40,000 income gap at 3 percent over the five-year Roth conversion period, their future income gap is revealed to be $46,371. In other words, to close their income gap in their sixth year of retirement, they'll need $46,371 of guaranteed lifetime income.

Step 4: Determine the Lump-Sum Contribution to the Fixed Indexed Annuity

Now that we know what Mike and Julie's guaranteed, inflation-adjusted income need is in year six of retirement, we can back into the contribution they'll need to make to their FIA at the outset.

This two-step process goes as follows:

Project a Growth Rate

The first step is to project a growth rate for the FIA during the Roth conversion period. Because the growth of the FIA is linked to the upward movement of a stock market index, the Smiths' initial contribution will have grown by the time they begin drawing their guaranteed lifetime income. The greater the anticipated growth rate over that five-year Roth conversion period, the less money they'll have to contribute to the FIA on day one. In the Smiths' case, we'll use an average growth rate of 4 percent per year.

The Guaranteed Lifetime Income Withdrawal Rate

The second critical variable that goes into calculating the initial contribution to the FIA is the guaranteed lifetime income withdrawal rate. This is the fixed percentage of income the Smiths can distribute from their FIA once they elect their lifetime income benefit. The longer they wait to draw this income, the greater their guaranteed lifetime income withdrawal rate. While percentages vary from company to company, a common withdrawal rate schedule might go as follows:

Age 61: 3.9 percent
Age 62: 4.1 percent
Age 63: 4.3 percent
Age 64: 4.5 percent
Age 65: 4.7 percent
Age 66: 4.9 percent
Age 67: 5.1 percent

As you can see, the longer the Smiths wait to draw a lifetime income, the higher the guaranteed lifetime income withdrawal rate once that income begins. Furthermore, the higher their guaranteed lifetime income withdrawal rate, the less they'll have to contribute to their FIA at the outset to create the income necessary to close their income gap by year six. Given their need for guaranteed lifetime income starting at age sixty-five, we can apply a withdrawal rate of 4.7 percent.

Calculating the Contribution to the Fixed Indexed Annuity

Now that we've established how these two variables work, we can calculate the FIA contribution required to meet the Smiths' inflation-adjusted income need by the end of their Roth conversion period. Given a 4 percent growth rate* over 5 years, and a 4.7 percent withdrawal rate at age 65, Mike and Julie would be required to make an initial contribution of $700,000† to their fixed indexed annuity in year one. Considering those variables, they could lock into roughly $46,000 of guaranteed income for life in their sixth year of retirement. And given the ongoing growth of the underlying indexes, this guaranteed income can keep pace with inflation over the course of the Smiths' retirement.

---

* A reminder that during the deferral period, some insurance companies offer premium bonuses and interest credit bonuses that apply to the income base from which the guaranteed lifetime income is computed. So even though an index might average only 4 percent per year, the net effect on the income base might be much higher than that.

† This amount varies by company and can be influenced by interest rates and mortality rates.

Step 5: Determine Annual Roth Conversion Amount

Because we want their guaranteed lifetime income to be 100 percent tax-free by year six, Mike and Julie will need to convert the entire $700,000 FIA over that 5-year time frame. Assuming the accumulation account grows at 4 percent per year, they'd need to convert about $157,000 per year. Now, while those annual conversions might seem large, they ensure the Smiths complete their Roth conversion before tax rates go up for good in 2026. More important, it keeps them in the 24 percent tax bracket. And by staying in the 24 percent bracket, they avoid having to pay taxes at the 28 percent bracket in 2026 when the tax sale of a lifetime draws unceremoniously to a close.

Step 6: Allocate Non-Annuity Assets to Time-Segmented Portfolios

A word of caution as we proceed into this section. The math here involves a lot of net present value calculations that can get complicated and messy. If you find this all a bit intimidating, don't lose hope! I'll be at your side, explaining and clarifying at every turn.

Ready? OK, let's dig in. Because it took only $700,000 to close Mike and Julie's income gap by year six, they still have $1.2 million to reallocate among their non-annuity investments. Mike and Julie currently have those dollars allocated in a traditional investment allocation of 50 percent stocks and 50 percent bonds. While such an allocation is less risky than a 100 percent stock market allocation, it won't eliminate sequence-of-return risk during that 5-year Roth conversion period.

Given the massive consequences of sequence-of-return risk, the Smiths should allocate their non-annuity assets based on the time-segmented allocation model described in chapter seven. The first step is to determine what portion of their non-annuity assets should be allocated to their cash account.

Cash Account (Year 1)

As a reminder, first-year expenses need to be paid out of a reliable account that isn't subject to the ebb and flow of the market. This account should be risk-free and guarantee their money will be there when they need it. For those reasons, a cash account is the ideal source from which to pay the Smiths' first-year expenses.

But how much money will the Smiths need to meet their cash flow needs in their first year of retirement? To determine this, they must first add the cost of their lifestyle needs, their LIRP contributions, and the Roth conversion amount for year one. This gives us their total gross income in their first year of retirement.

Lifestyle need	$80,000
LIRP contributions	$45,000
Roth conversion	$157,000
Total gross income in year 1	$282,000

Their total gross income for year one of retirement is $282,000. This is an important number because it helps us calculate the Smiths' total tax liability. Once we know their total year one tax liability, we can add that amount to the cash account as well.

Calculating the Tax

The first step in determining their year one tax liability is to determine their effective tax rate. This is the actual tax rate they'll have to pay on their entire gross income. This can be done with the help of an online effective tax calculator.

A quick calculation reveals that $282,000 of gross income yields a total federal effective tax rate of 17.7 percent. Throw in another 5 percent for state tax, and that brings their total effective tax rate to 22.7 percent. This means they'll need to allocate $64,014 for taxes their first year of retirement.

Now that we know the Smiths' total tax liability, we can calculate their total cash flow need for their first year of retirement. Remember, their $157,000 Roth conversion is not a cash flow need and does not need to be accounted for in this calculation.

Lifestyle need	$80,000
LIRP contributions	$45,000
Total tax obligation	$64,014
Total cash requirement	$189,014

So, the total that needs to be allocated to their cash account for year one is $189,014. The next question that naturally arises is: From which bucket(s) will the Smiths distribute money to meet this total cash flow need?

Pay Taxes from Your Taxable Bucket

It's important to remember that whenever possible, you should pay your taxes out of your taxable bucket. By doing so, you use your least valuable bucket (taxable) as a catalyst to shift your second least valuable bucket (tax-deferred) into your most valuable bucket (tax-free). This approach can help you maximize the amount of money you accumulate and ultimately distribute from your tax-free bucket.

In the Smiths' case, they have $400,000 in their taxable bucket. This far exceeds the ideal balance for an emergency fund and is more than enough to pay for their tax obligations over the course of their five-year Roth conversion period. By paying their taxes out of their taxable bucket, they can whittle this balance down to a more manageable amount by the time they begin drawing their guaranteed lifetime income in year six. In doing so, they shrink this bucket's tax obligations, which increases the likelihood they'll reach the 0 percent tax bracket by the time the Roth conversion period is over.

Incidentally, if the Smiths didn't have the luxury of paying for their taxes out of their taxable bucket, they'd have to take even larger distributions from their tax-deferred bucket to compensate for the additional taxation.

In summary, the Smiths will shift $64,014 from their taxable investments to their cash account in year one to pay for taxes. They'll liquidate an additional $125,000 from their non-annuity IRAs and transfer that to their cash account as well.*

Total allocation to cash: $189,014

Now that we've satisfied the Smiths' cash flow needs in their first year of retirement, let's discuss how to allocate the balance of their portfolios in years two through five and beyond.

---

* Tax payments in years two through five will continue to be drawn from the Smiths' taxable buckets, while their lifestyle expenses will continue to be funded from their IRAs.

Portfolio 1 (Years 2 and 3)

Because the Smiths won't need to access the money in Portfolio 1 for at least a year, they can afford to take *some* risk with this money. They want to take precisely the amount of risk that corresponds to this one- to two-year time horizon. If they can grow this money at 2.5 percent per year, they can stay within shouting distance of inflation.

The Smiths don't want to allocate any more money to this portfolio than is required to meet their cash flow needs in years two and three of retirement. Every dollar that is unnecessarily allocated to a 2.5 percent portfolio is one less dollar that can be allocated to the high-octane, aggressive-growth portfolio reserved for all post–Roth conversion investment dollars.

We can ensure that the amount we contribute to this portfolio is precisely the right amount by performing several calculations.

First, the Smiths must determine the amount of money they'll need at the beginning of years two and three to pay for their inflation-adjusted lifestyle needs. Assuming an annual inflation rate of 3 percent, they'll need $82,400 at the beginning of year two and $84,872 at the beginning of year three, for a total of $167,272.

Second, we add in $90,000 ($45,000 x 2) to fully fund their respective LIRPs for both years.

Finally, we calculate the taxes on their lifestyle, LIRP contributions, and $157,000 Roth conversions for each year. That total equals $64,558 for year two and $65,119 for year three. That means their total cash flow needs are $191,958 for year two and $194,991 for year three.

Next, we perform a net present value calculation on that total—the total of $191,958 and $194,991, which are from years 2 and 3—to determine the deposit necessary in year one to achieve the required distributions by the beginning of years two and three, given that 2.5 percent annual growth rate. A quick net present value calculation (a financial planning calculator comes in handy here) gives us the answer: $372,871.

Total allocation to Portfolio 1: $372,871

Portfolio 2 (Years 4 and 5)

Now that we've laid the philosophical foundation for how to allocate dollars toward Portfolio 1, the allocation for Portfolio 2 is easier to calculate. We apply the same 3 percent inflation rate to their lifestyle need, only this time over three and four years, respectively. Assuming a growth rate of 3.5 percent on the assets in Portfolio 2, we can then perform the same net present value calculation to determine the amount of money the Smiths need to deposit in year one to yield the appropriate balances by years four and five. When we perform all of these calculations, we determine the total allocation to Portfolio 2 to be $354,139.

Total allocation to Portfolio 2: $354,139

Upon seeing the total cashflow requirements for years one through five, your first-blush response might be, *"Wow, that's an expensive way for the Smiths to spend the first five years of their retirement!"* While this seems true on the surface, let's step back and appreciate the broader picture.

First, the cash required to meet their lifestyle needs is unusually high because the Smiths have yet to draw their Social Security. By postponing receipt of their Social Security until age sixty-five, they lock into a much higher benefit. In essence, they're spending more of their assets in the short term to guarantee higher, tax-free, inflation-adjusted Social Security payments over the long term.

Second, the $45,000 annual LIRP contribution should not be considered an expense. Rather, it should be understood in the same light as the Roth conversion. The Smiths are merely repositioning a portion of their IRA to the LIRP, where it can grow safely and productively, and ultimately provide them with a death benefit that doubles as long-term care. What's more, the LIRP will be a reliable source of tax-free income over the balance of the Smiths' retirement.

Lastly, if the tax liability seems large, it's because we've intentionally made it so. The Smiths are *preemptively* paying taxes at historically low tax rates on their own terms, so the IRS can't force them to pay tax rates on the federal government's terms somewhere down the road when they really need the cash. And don't forget the silver lining: by shifting their money over a five-year period, the Smiths stay within the 24 percent tax bracket. Ten years from now they will look back at that 24 percent tax bracket as a good deal of historic proportions.

In short, the cash outlays during the Roth conversion period may seem unwieldy, but they're calculated to permanently remove tax rate risk and longevity risk from the Smiths' retirement by the first day of their sixth year of retirement.*

Portfolio 5 (Post–Roth Conversion Portfolio)

Any of the Smiths' assets not earmarked for Portfolios 1 and 2 get allocated to Portfolio 5.† Remember, Portfolio 5 is

---

* Now consider a scenario in which the Smiths have even larger IRAs. In that case, they might choose to convert their IRAs over a longer period of time, perhaps seven to ten years. Were this the case, they'd need to allocate a portion of their non-annuity assets to Portfolios 3 and 4 discussed in the previous chapter. Given the longer time horizons, these portfolios would be invested in bond instruments that have longer maturities and even higher yields.

† Because the Smiths' Roth conversion took place over five years, Portfolios 3 and 4 were not needed.

a high-octane, aggressive-growth portfolio earmarked for discretionary needs once the Roth conversion period is complete. When the Smiths start drawing their guaranteed lifetime income in year six, they won't be constrained to take distributions from their stock portfolio when the market is down. This allows them to take much more risk than they might otherwise have taken were they solely reliant on this portfolio to meet their lifestyle needs.

To determine the allocation to Portfolio 5, we simply add all the assets that have been allocated to cash, Portfolio 1, and Portfolio 2, and subtract that from the Smiths' total non-annuity investments. Remember, in step 4, we allocated $700,000 to the fixed indexed annuity, leaving us with $1.2 million of non-annuity assets. When we add the balances in cash, Portfolio 1, and Portfolio 2, we get $916,024. We then subtract that figure from their total non-annuity assets of $1,200,000. That leaves them with $283,976. That's the portion of their portfolio that gets allocated to Portfolio 5 on their first day of retirement.

Incidentally, should the money in Portfolio 5 average 5 percent net of fees during the Roth conversion period, they'd have closer to $360,000 by the time they draw their guaranteed lifetime income. Furthermore, they will have contributed $225,000 to their LIRPs over that same time frame. Barring any major shock expenses in the meantime, these two accounts could have over $750,000 in cash by the time the Smiths reach age 70. That's a robust pool of tax-free capital that can be easily tapped to pay for discretionary expenses over the balance of their retirement.

Note that when the Smiths reach age 72, they'll have to start taking required minimum distributions. These distributions start at 3.91 percent of their cumulative IRA balances and go up from there. It's critical that the Smiths monitor the growth of their IRAs to ensure their balances stay low enough that their RMDs are equal to or less than their standard deduction *and* low enough that they don't cause Social Security taxation. Should the growth of the Smiths' IRAs put them on track to produce excessively large RMDs by age 72, they can perform preemptive Roth conversions along the way.

Total allocation to Portfolio 5: $283,976

By completing this six-step process, the Smiths will have created four different streams of tax-free income that land them in the 0 percent tax bracket by their sixth year of retirement. These four tax-free streams of income are as follows:

Roth conversion: This inflation-adjusted, tax-free stream of income comes from the Smiths' fixed indexed annuity.

LIRP: Tax-free income from the LIRP is most impactful when accessed in the eleventh policy year and beyond.

Required minimum distributions: So long as the Smiths take distributions from their remaining IRAs that are equal to or less than their standard deduction in a given year, these distributions are likewise tax-free.

Social Security: Provided the Smiths stay below their provisional income threshold, they receive their Social Security 100 percent tax-free. This requires that they closely monitor their IRA balances and distributions along the way.

Let's not forget that they also eliminated longevity risk by electing a guaranteed, tax-free stream of income from their fixed indexed annuity in year six.

IN SUMMARY

Let's review the step-by-step process designed to shield the Smiths from higher taxes in the future *and* eliminate longevity risk from their retirement picture:

Step 1: We sent the Smiths through the qualification process for the LIRP. This accomplished two things: it helped predict their life expectancies and it corroborated the viability of the LIRP strategy. We also determined that an annual contribution of $45,000 over 5 years would give each of them roughly $400,000 of death benefit. Thanks to the LIRP's chronic-illness rider, they could each receive $100,000 per year over 4 years for the purpose of paying for long-term care.*

Step 2: Upon approval of the Smiths' LIRPs, we put their policies in force by contributing a total of $45,000 in the first year. This secured their death benefits and gave them long-term coverage. This also provided them a pool of liquid capital that can be accessed beginning in policy year eleven and beyond to pay for discretionary expenses.

Step 3: We calculated the Smiths' income gap for the year immediately following their Roth conversion period. We did this by subtracting their lifestyle need ($80,000) from their anticipated Social Security benefit at age 65 ($40,000). We then inflated this number over 5 years to determine the size of their income gap in year six. This amount was $46,371.

---

* This amount may be discounted based on the age at which they elect the chronic illness benefit.

Step 4: By using a growth rate of 4 percent and an anticipated withdrawal rate of 4.7 percent, we determined the Smiths would need to contribute $700,000 to their fixed indexed annuity in year one of retirement.*

Step 5: In order to completely transition their FIA to tax-free, we determined that the Smiths needed to do a $157,000 Roth conversion every year for five years. This provides them a guaranteed, tax-free, inflation-adjusted stream of income starting in year six of retirement. Coupled with their Social Security, this income is designed to completely remove longevity risk from their retirement picture.

Step 6: Because of the disproportionate threat of sequence-of-return risk during the five-year Roth conversion period, we allocated their liquid investments among a cash account and three additional time-segmented portfolios. The cash account is designed to cover their lifestyle expenses, LIRP contributions, and taxes during their first year of retirement. The capital required for the Smiths' cash flow needs in years two

---

* A reminder that during the deferral period, some insurance companies offer premium bonuses and interest credit bonuses that apply to the income base from which the guaranteed lifetime income is computed. So even though an index might average only 4 percent per year, the net effect on the income base might be much higher than that.

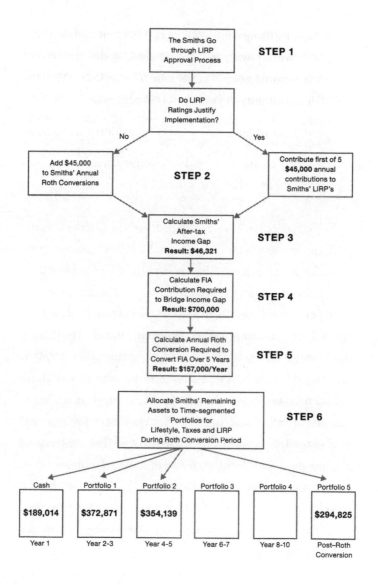

through five was allocated to Portfolios 1 and 2. These portfolios are designed to provide safe and productive returns while shielding the Smiths from the insidious effects of sequence-of-return risk. Any assets not allocated to these three accounts were allocated to Portfolio 5. This high-octane, aggressive-growth portfolio is designed to fund their discretionary needs once the Roth conversion period is over.

By completing this six-step process, the Smiths accomplish three important things. First, by repositioning a portion of their tax-deferred dollars in the tax-free bucket, they create multiple sources of tax-free income that land them in the 0 percent tax bracket and shield them from tax rate risk. Second, by choosing a fixed indexed annuity that has a piecemeal internal Roth conversion feature, they create a tax-free, inflation-adjusted stream of income that is guaranteed to last as long as they do. Lastly, by funding the high-octane Portfolio 5 and their LIRPs, they'll have a substantial pool of tax-free capital designed to meet all their discretionary income needs over the course of their retirement.

It took a bit of heavy lifting along the way, but by the time the dust settled, the Smiths emerged with a dynamic, proactive retirement strategy that shields them from tax rate risk *and* longevity risk!

Chapter 9

CONCLUSION

For decades retirement experts have studied the two greatest threats to your retirement happiness: tax rate risk and longevity risk. And while strategists in each camp have provided thoughtful, proactive, math-based solutions to these threats, their dueling approaches often cancel each other out. In the very act of mitigating one risk, they compound the consequences of the other. Consider the financial adviser who recommends you bridge your retirement income gap with a single premium immediate annuity within your tax-deferred bucket. While such an approach *can* help you successfully mitigate longevity risk, it permanently exposes you to the risk of rising taxes and Social Security taxation. Regardless of which risk your financial plan ignores, the result is always the same: you're forced to spend down your liquid assets to compensate. And that increases the likelihood that you run out of money before you die.

A truly comprehensive, *Tax-Free Income for Life* approach to retirement planning, on the other hand, fully mitigates both these insidious retirement risks in a harmonious and synergistic way. By positioning the ideal amount of assets in each of your three investment buckets, you remove the IRS from your retirement equation, regardless of the future of tax rates. And by utilizing a fixed indexed annuity with a piecemeal internal Roth conversion feature, you can shift your assets to the tax-free bucket *and* lock in a stream of income guaranteed to last as long as you do. Furthermore, by supplementing this approach with an LIRP and a time-segmented approach to investing, you can neutralize a wide array of additional risks that you're certain to encounter along your retirement journey.

Now, I know what you're thinking right about now. It's much easier to *talk* about a comprehensive *Tax-Free Income for Life* retirement strategy than to put one in place. I will concede that the approach I've outlined in this book requires more proactive effort and patience than the traditional, reflexive, tax-deferred approach to retirement planning. It's much easier to adopt a financial plan that omits fixed indexed annuities, Roth conversions, and LIRPs. There'd be no need to compute your inflation-adjusted lifestyle needs at the end of your Roth conversion period so you can determine the precise contribution to the FIA required to guarantee your lifetime expenses. You wouldn't have to perform complicated net present value calculations within strategic time-segmented portfolios. You could simply leave all your assets in your IRA or 401(k), take distributions as needed, and *hope* your money lasts until you die.

And while such an approach might be less complicated and time-intensive in the short term, it's sure to add wrinkles to your skin and gray to your hair over time. Here's the bottom line: if you want to completely eliminate the two greatest risks to your retirement plan, you're going to have to put in some extra effort. It's going to require more planning, a bit more complexity, and a dynamic, forward-thinking strategy.

All this leads to my next point. It's challenging to navigate the road to the 0 percent tax bracket without the aid of a seasoned expert who's trod this path before. Violate a threshold on the one hand and you'll pay an extra tax on the other. Accumulate too many dollars in either the taxable or tax-deferred bucket and you'll miss the 0 percent tax bracket altogether *and* give up a hefty portion of your Social Security along the way. Before you know it, you've depleted your retirement portfolio twelve to fifteen years faster than you ever thought possible. In short, there are dozens of pitfalls that stand between you and the 0 percent tax bracket. When you add in strategies designed to fully mitigate *longevity risk* as well, the complexity of your financial plan compounds even further.

Because of this increased complexity, it's critical you find a qualified financial adviser to shepherd you through this retirement planning process. But a word of caution: it's not enough to engage an adviser who is adept at mitigating only *one* of these retirement risks. Should they fail to mitigate *both* risks, you could find yourself hemorrhaging money at a point in your retirement when you can least afford to do so. It's imperative that you engage a qualified financial guide who is adept at eliminating *both* risks *within the very same financial plan.*

How can you find such an expert? Begin by talking with the person who gave you this book. Ask them how these principles apply to your situation. Request that they analyze your financial scenario and lay out a customized, step-by-step strategy designed to eliminate tax rate risk *and* longevity risk from your retirement picture. If that strategy is clear, detailed, and mathematical, then they pass the first test. If that adviser is likewise committed to investing the necessary time to execute your plan (remember, this approach can take up to ten years to fully implement), then you've likely found a worthy partner in your retirement journey.

If you are unable to find an expert who satisfies these criteria, go to davidmcknight.com, and we'll be happy to connect you with a qualified, experienced adviser in your area.

Thank you for the trust you've placed in me as we've navigated the intricacies of a *Tax-Free Income for Life* retirement plan. I wish you all the peace and prosperity you so richly deserve as you embark on this exciting retirement journey.

Chapter 10

FREQUENTLY ASKED
QUESTIONS

O ver the years I've been asked a number of questions about how to alleviate tax rate risk and longevity risk within the same financial plan. What follows is a list of the most relevant questions divided by category. Ultimately, the best way to answer the questions that pertain to your specific situation is to consult with a qualified financial adviser.

FIXED INDEXED ANNUITIES

Q: What are the risks of waiting to start my FIA?

A: If you recall, guaranteed lifetime income withdrawal rates are a function of interest rates and life expectancy. By waiting to start an FIA, you run the risk that Americans extend their life expectances or that interest rates go down. Either scenario would lower the guaranteed withdrawal percentage of your annuity.

Q: Why is the withdrawal rate on an FIA lower than the withdrawal rate on an SPIA?

A: The FIA affords you benefits that you won't find in the SPIA, namely liquidity, inflation protection, and a death benefit. Insurance companies pay for these additional benefits by lowering your guaranteed withdrawal percentage.

Q: Should I elect guaranteed lifetime income over a single life or joint life?

A: Insurance companies typically give you a choice between taking guaranteed income over your life and over the joint life of you and your spouse. Because the life expectancy of two people is longer than that of one, your guaranteed withdrawal rate is reduced if you choose the joint life option, typically by about half a percent. For this reason, it makes sense to elect the single life option on the spouse with the longer life expectancy. This will allow you to increase the cumulative withdrawals you take over the life of the annuity. One of the best ways to determine which of the two spouses is going to live longer is to go through the LIRP underwriting process.

Q: Can I utilize the fixed indexed annuity as a bond replacement?

A: Even if you never use the FIA for its guaranteed lifetime income feature, it can still serve as a bond alternative. In fact, the FIA is superior to a traditional bond portfolio because of insurance companies' massive economies of scale. Annuity expert Tom Hegna says annuities perform like CCC bonds with AAA ratings. Also, FIAs have a standard deviation of zero,* which means you can get higher rates of return without the risk of a traditional bond portfolio. Furthermore, by replacing the bond portion of your retirement portfolio with an FIA, you can increase the risk in the stock portion of your retirement savings without increasing the standard deviation of the overall portfolio.

Q: What are the benefits of beginning my annuity before I retire?

---

* Standard deviation is a statistical measurement of investment volatility.

A: By implementing your annuity before you retire, you can get a head start on your Roth conversion before tax rates go up for good. Furthermore, you won't have to spend down any of your stock market portfolio to support your lifestyle during the Roth conversion period. In a perfect world, you would complete the Roth conversion of your FIA in the year just prior to your retirement. This would require you to begin the strategy between two and ten years prior to your retirement date, depending on the amount of Roth conversions your retirement plan calls for.

Q: Can my account value go negative when factoring in the extra charge for the guaranteed income rider?

A: Remember, some annuity companies charge around 1 percent for the guaranteed lifetime income rider. That rider cost gets applied to your accumulation value every year, so, in theory, a series of negative returns in the underlying index could cause your accumulation value to go negative. While this is the case with some annuities, others guarantee that your accumulation value will never go negative, regardless of the performance of the underlying index.

Q: Does it ever make sense to keep the annuity within the tax-deferred bucket?

A: It is possible to create an inflation-adjusted stream of lifetime income within the tax-deferred bucket designed to keep pace with your standard deduction. Using your inflation-adjusted standard deduction to offset this income would ensure that it would always be tax-free. However, because provisional income thresholds don't adjust for inflation, this approach would almost certainly cause your Social Security to be taxed within the first ten years of your retirement. Your inflation-adjusted annuity income would eventually eclipse the provisional income thresholds, at which point at least 50 percent of your Social Security would be taxable. Furthermore, if the lifetime income generated by your annuity is required to stay below your standard deduction ($24,800 for married couples in 2020)* for tax purposes, it may not be sufficient to close your retirement income gap.

ROTH CONVERSIONS

Q: What is the five-year rule with the Roth conversion?

A: If you do a Roth conversion before you are age 59.5, you will have to wait five years or until 59.5, whichever comes first, before you can touch the principal without penalty. If

---

* Married filing jointly

you're already 59.5 when you make the conversion, you can withdraw the principal immediately, but you'll have to wait five years (measured from the tax year of your first contribution or conversion to any Roth IRA) before you touch any of the earnings without being subject to income tax.

Q: What happens if my Roth conversion extends beyond 2025?

A: In 2026, tax rates will return to where they were in 2017. Should your Roth conversion strategy spill into 2026 and beyond, you will pay more tax on those converted dollars. But keep in mind, it may still make sense to pay taxes at those somewhat higher rates if it spares you from paying double the rates somewhere down the road.

Q: Can I pay the taxes on my Roth conversion out of the tax-deferred bucket?

A: It is always ideal to pay taxes on your Roth conversion out of the taxable bucket when possible. This especially makes sense when you're converting money within your fixed indexed annuity. Your goal should be to preserve 100 percent of that guaranteed, tax-free lifetime income in retirement. However, in some cases, you may be required to pay taxes on your Roth conversion from your existing IRAs. If that's the case, you're better off paying those taxes from your non-annuity IRAs than from the fixed indexed annuity itself.

Q: Does it still make sense to convert my fixed indexed annuity if it forces me to spend down some of my liquid retirement savings in the meantime?

A: In short, yes. Remember, the Roth conversion of your FIA forces you to postpone the election of your guaranteed lifetime income. And the longer you wait to elect that income, the higher your withdrawal rate when you do so. This allows you to make a smaller contribution to the FIA at the beginning of the Roth conversion period. So, even though the Roth conversion forces you to spend down some of your liquid assets along the way, it allows you to make a smaller contribution to the FIA at the outset.

Q: Does the Roth conversion have income limitations?

A: Anyone can do a Roth conversion, regardless of income level.

Q: How quickly should I convert my IRA?

A: You should convert your IRA quickly enough that you pay the taxes owed before tax rates rise dramatically, but slowly enough that you don't bump yourself into a tax bracket that gives you heartburn.

LIFE INSURANCE RETIREMENT PLAN (LIRP)

Q: How soon can I touch my money?

A: LIRPs generally have a surrender period or vesting schedule, similar to a 401(k). This schedule exists because life insurance companies incur substantial expenses when getting these programs up and running. By putting a surrender period in place, they reserve the right to recuperate those expenses should you decide to cash in the policy during that time frame.

Q: What happens if I run out of money in my LIRP before I die?

A: You want to avoid this scenario at all costs. If you don't have at least one dollar in your LIRP's cash value at death, the taxes you avoided along the way will come due all in one year. One way to avoid this outcome is to make sure your LIRP has a provision known as an over-loan protection rider.

Q: Can the LIRP really cover cash flow needs and long-term care needs in retirement?

A: Yes, but this requires that you balance each of these competing objectives. As we discussed, life insurance companies give you access to your death benefit in advance of your death for the purpose of paying for long-term care. Your death benefit consists of your cash value plus whatever amount of life insurance you're paying for in a given year (see my book *Look Before You LIRP* for a deeper discussion of this topic). So if you spend down too much of your cash value before you need long-term care, you can decimate the pool of money from which the long-term care benefits are derived. A qualified financial adviser can help you understand how to moderate the distributions from your LIRP and still have a robust pool of funds from which to pay long-term care expenses.

Q: Why is it best to wait ten years before accessing the cash value of my LIRP?

A: This is a question of LIRP expenses. The LIRP has higher expenses in the early years and lower expenses in the later years. When you average these expenses out over your full retirement, however, they can cost as little as 1 percent of your bucket per year. Because of the front-loaded nature of its fees, the LIRP needs time to marinate. If you start accessing the LIRP's cash value too early, it can stymie the momentum of its growth account. By the eleventh year, this account has built a sufficient head of steam and will be large enough to cover important discretionary expenses.

TIME-SEGMENTED INVESTING

Q: Will the lower returns in Portfolios 1 through 4 hamper the growth of my overall portfolio?

A: Even though you're getting lower returns in these bond-heavy portfolios, Portfolio 5 has a 100 percent stock allocation. When taken as a whole, these five portfolios operate like a traditional, diversified portfolio. By the end of your Roth conversion period, however, you will have likely depleted all the assets in Portfolios 1 through 4, leaving your overall portfolio disproportionately weighted toward stocks. At this point, your guaranteed lifetime income and your LIRP can function as the bond portion of your portfolio, allowing you to maintain your aggressive stock allocation within Portfolio 5.

Q: How do I determine how much money to allocate to each portfolio?

A: You can calculate the required contributions to each portfolio with the help of a financial calculator with a net present value function. If you need help with these calculations, talk to the adviser who gave you this book. If you don't have an adviser, you can get help with these calculations at davidmcknight.com.

Q: What if I have money left over in Portfolios 1 through 4 at the end of a given time segment?

A: Any money not spent during a given time segment should be rolled into the aggressive-growth allocation in Portfolio 5. For example, let's assume that by the end of year three, you have $20,000 left over in Portfolio 1. These surplus funds should be immediately diverted to Portfolio 5, where they can grow much more aggressively.

SOCIAL SECURITY

Q: When should I draw Social Security with this strategy?

A: The question of when to draw Social Security comes down to life expectancy. The longer you're likely to live, the longer you should defer Social Security benefits. It generally doesn't make sense to draw Social Security during the Roth conversion period, as the additional provisional income will cause those benefits to be taxed. Defer your Social Security until the end of the conversion period so you can lock into a higher, tax-free amount. If you want further clarity on your life expectancy, it may make sense to go through the LIRP qualification process.

CREATING A FINANCIAL LEGACY FOR HEIRS

Q: How does this strategy impact my beneficiaries?

A: Passing money in the tax-deferred bucket to your children can create a cascade of negative tax consequences. If you're close to retirement age, you'll not likely pass this money to your children for at least twenty years. When they do inherit this money, it will be at the apex of their earning years, at a time when tax rates are likely to be much higher than they are today. As a result, your heirs could end up losing 50 percent or more of your IRA to tax—probably not how you wanted your hard-earned retirement savings to be spent. By repositioning your assets to tax-free accounts during your lifetime, you pay taxes at historically low rates so that your children can spend the money tax-free at a time in their lives when they could really use a tax-free infusion of cash.

Q: How does the SECURE Act of 2019 impact this strategy?

A: The big change brought about by the SECURE Act of 2019 is the death of the stretch IRA. Your non-spouse beneficiaries (i.e., your children) will no longer be allowed to take required minimum distributions on inherited IRAs over their own life expectancies. Instead, they'll be required to pay tax on the full inherited IRA amount within ten years.* Let's illustrate the tax implications of this change by using the example of a $1 million inherited IRA growing at 6.5 percent per year. To liquidate this account by the end of that ten-year period, your beneficiary would be forced to

---

* Roth IRAs have to be spent down within ten years as well, but without any tax ramifications along the way.

realize roughly $140,000 of income per year. That income would be piled right on top of all their other income and be taxed at their highest marginal tax rate. So if you're equivocating over a Roth conversion while you're alive because you don't want to pay taxes at your current rates, consider the rates your children would have to pay during that ten-year period of condensed taxation.

AND LAST BUT NOT LEAST . . .

Q: How will my life improve if I adopt a *Tax-Free Income for Life* retirement strategy?

A: You'll live an appreciably longer life, likely deep into your nineties, maintain a lithe and youthful physique, compound your marital bliss, receive visits from your grandchildren with dizzying frequency, and live the quintessentially happy retirement, the most vexing challenge of which will be how to spend that stubborn, guaranteed lifetime paycheck month after glorious month.

I invite you to learn more at davidmcknight.com.

ACKNOWLEDGMENTS

My deepest, most heartfelt thanks go to . . .

—My indefatigable agent, Howard Yoon, who found a home for this book, even as he cradled a newborn baby in the crook of his arm.

—My editor, Noah Schwartzberg, whose keen eye for detail helped chip off this manuscript's rough edges and turn it into a polished final product.

—Tom Hegna, the greatest advocate for guaranteed lifetime income this country has ever known.

—Ed Slott, CPA, who has been warning against the inevitability of higher taxes and advocating for tax-free investing for the last twenty years.

—Van Mueller, my fellow Wisconsinite who is a tireless advocate for the tax-free planning paradigm as a safeguard against the fiscal storm bearing down on our country.

—Larry DeLegge, who served as a key sounding board throughout this entire process.

—Maxwell Waletich, who spent valuable time brainstorming with me on how to make the case studies in this book come to life.

—Kyle Swann, CFP, whose encyclopedic knowledge of financial planning gave this book the technical rigor it required.

—A long list of savvy financial advisors who gave valuable time reviewing the manuscript and made important and indispensable contributions.

—The vast network of Power of Zero advisors across the nation whose proactive efforts help shield their clients from the effects of tax-rate risk and longevity risk.

—Most important, my wife, Felice, whose tireless work within the walls of our home makes a deep and lasting impact on the world.